TROPICAL FISH

A guide for setting up and maintaining
an aquarium for tropical fish and other animals

by BRUCE W. HALSTEAD
and BONNIE L. LANDA
illustrated by GEORGE SANDSTROM

 GOLDEN PRESS · NEW YORK

Western Publishing Company, Inc.
Racine, Wisconsin

FOREWORD

Few animals provide the profusion of colors, diversity of form, and beauty of movement offered by aquatic life, particularly tropical fish. Establishing and maintaining an aquarium offers an insight into the complexities of the natural world—an exciting and rewarding opportunity to observe ecological principles in operation. Ecology is the science that deals with the relationship of animals and plants to their environment and to each other, and these dynamic environmental forces can be seen clearly in an aquarium. On a larger scale, similar environmental factors control mankind's destiny, for today's world faces unprecedented problems and challenges in maintaining a balance of nature.

This book was written to help hobbyists with one of the most exciting and educational of all sparetime pursuits: studying a closed ecological system in an aquarium. The fish and other organisms described and illustrated in this book were selected largely on the basis of their availability, beauty, and general interest. Those who master the basic principles of maintaining aquariums will probably find it challenging to experiment with animals (and plants) not included in this brief manual. The aquarium hobby truly has no limits.

B.W.H.
B. L. L.

Credits: Mel Venti, Chester County Aqua-Pet, Inc., Paoli, Pa., and John R. Paxson, Exton Hardware Store in Exton, Pa., for providing specimens for the artist.

CONTENTS

TROPICAL FISH

Ever since the first Goldfish was kept captive in China, more than a thousand years ago, the keeping of fish has grown steadily in popularity. The demands and curiosity on the part of enthusiasts during the last few decades has resulted in more information and equipment becoming available for the millions of hobbyists all over the world.

Stresses and problems of everyday living are easily forgotten as you watch underwater spectacles in your own living room. An aquarium stocked with fish and plants provides lasting and continuous entertainment, and the gratification that comes from creating your own miniature underwater world is without compare.

Fish are unique pets. They do not make noises, run away, eat large amounts of food, or chew up your favorite pair of slippers. For the price of only one or two cans of pet food, you can buy a beautiful tropical fish. Landlords who prohibit other pets generally allow aquariums. Many owners have taught their pets to eat from their fingers or to swim to the surface to rest in their hand or to be petted. If their offspring are raised and sold, pets can more than pay for their room and board.

An aquarium adds to a home's decor, and its maintenance is not difficult. The aquarium should be arranged with care prior to purchasing any fish.

When ecological principles are being considered seriously, establishing and maintaining an aquarium becomes much more than a simple hobby. Ordinarily only qualified technicians can study these

An aquarium adds live entertainment to a room's decor.

closed systems and then apply their findings to the outside world. Experienced, professional aquaculturists raise fish by the millions in large outside tanks as a source of food for humans. This is a possible way to increase the available protein for undernourished peoples.

5

Buy the largest tank possible. In general, the more space fish have, the better they do. Also, it is much easier to keep a large tank clean. Different species vary in their activities, growth, and space demands. As examples, ten baby Guppies require considerably less space than ten of the smallest Goldfish. Keep in mind, too, that it is almost impossible to resist adding new inhabitants to the tank, and so extra volume is soon utilized.

The smallest tank in which one should invest is ten gallons. If a new tank is too expensive for the budget, look for a bargain in newspaper ads or at auctions. An inexpensive or second-hand aquarium may leak, but it can be resealed.

NON-TOXIC SEALANT should be used to prevent or stop leaks. Often the seepage may be in the inside top corner, but the water leaks out the opposite bottom outside seam. Excess sealant can be trimmed off with a razor blade. Be careful not to scratch the glass or plastic.

Put the aquarium in a dry, clean place and allow the sealer to dry and set for at least two weeks. Then age the aquarium in aerated water for another week before using it. Leaks in an old aquarium can sometimes be sealed by filling the tank slowly with hot water.

Seal all seams of aquarium with sealant that can be bought in a pet shop.

AQUARIUMS

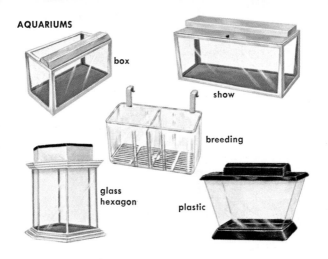

box

show

breeding

glass hexagon

plastic

SIZES AND SHAPES of aquariums vary. Rectangular tanks with stainless-steel frames and glass sides are the kind most recommended. These are relatively shallow tanks, providing the greatest surface area per volume of water for the exchange of oxygen and carbon dioxide. If a glass pane is broken, it can be replaced. Tanks made of all glass cannot be repaired. Plastic aquariums are easily scratched, and with age the panes sometimes become discolored. Wooden tanks must be emptied, dried, and recoated with resin from time to time.

GALLON VOLUME of a rectangular tank is determined by the formula (in inches) below:

$$\frac{width \times length \times height}{231}$$

This volume must be known when it is necessary to add medicines to the water. Ornaments and gravel take up space. If they are already in place, it may be easiest to measure the volume of water as the tank is being filled. Note this figure and keep it where it will not be lost.

LOCATION must be decided before selecting the kind and size of aquarium. Keep in mind that each gallon of water weighs approximately 8⅓ pounds, so the stand must be sturdy. Its location must be permanent, the surface level. Moving or tilting a tank that is even partially full of water or gravel often results in leaks.

5 teaspoons of salt to 1 gallon of water disinfects and cleans

AVOID having to use extension cords. Put the aquarium near an electrical outlet. Do not place the aquarium on top of a television set or a hi-fi, where the water may overheat and kill the plants and animals. In too much light, green algae thrive on the glass and in the water. The algae do not harm the fish but are not attractive. Controlling algae can be a constant struggle, so locate tank away from windows.

The temperature of the room should be constant, and there should be no drafts. The air must be clean. Insecticides, household sprays, paint fumes, and tobacco smoke can be dangerous to fish and plants.

BE SANITARY. Before working with the aquarium, wash your hands with soap. Rinse repeatedly. Scrub the soap and dirt from under your fingernails with a stiff brush. Rinse all the way up your arm if it will be submerged. Then rinse your hands and equipment in a strong salt solution, which both cleans and disinfects. Finally, rinse again with fresh water. Never allow cleansers or hand lotions near tanks.

TO SIPHON, fill the tube (old hose or plastic tube) full of water. Hold a thumb over each end of the tube. Put one end in the aquarium water and make sure the other end is below the level of the tube in the aquarium. Now remove the thumbs, and the water should flow freely. A siphoning tube made especially for aquariums can be purchased at a pet store.

TEST A NEW TANK FOR LEAKAGE before you put it in place. This test will prevent the soaking of valuable furniture and rugs. The guarantee on a new tank may be honored, but a warped piece of furniture or a stained rug are not covered by the guarantee.

Select a waterproof surface where cool water can be hosed or poured into the tank. Be sure the bottom of the tank is dry before filling it, or you will not be able to determine if the tank is really leaking. Allow the tank to sit for at least twelve hours.

After the test, scoop or siphon the water from the tank. Do not lift the tank with weight inside it. Rinse with a salt solution. Even though tank does not leak, aquarium may sweat at first. Put waterproof material under aquarium to catch this moisture.

FILTRATION

Filtration, if the unit is properly operated, saves hours of cleaning. By providing a greater surface area for oxygen to enter the tank, filtering also increases fish capacity. There are two basic types of filters: charcoal-floss and undergravel.

A CORNER FILTER, located inside the aquarium, is a plastic box containing aquarium charcoal (also called carbon) on the lower half and filter floss on the top. The charcoal cleans the water and absorbs many impurities; the floss removes debris. Water is circulated through these two, which become soiled and must be changed every two weeks.

Always rinse new charcoal thoroughly. Store unused dry carbon in an airtight container where it cannot absorb poisons from the air. Activated high-quality charcoals may be cleaned and reused several times by simply rinsing and drying them in a clean place.

Buy filter floss, not glass wool. Particles of glass can lodge in and injure the fish's gills or can be transferred to people's eyes from their hands. Never pack the floss into a filter. This reduces the operating efficiency of the filter and puts a strain on the pump.

CORNER FILTER

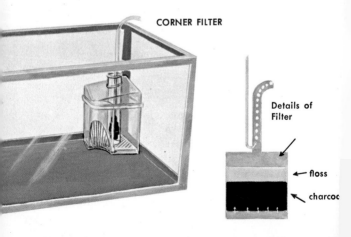

Details of Filter

← floss

← charcoal

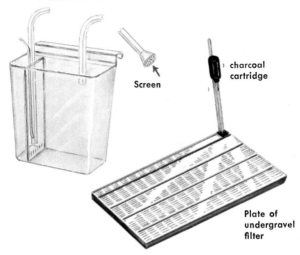

OUTSIDE FILTER

Screen

charcoal
cartridge

Plate of
undergravel
filter

AN OUTSIDE FILTER is also a plastic box, with floss in the upper half and charcoal in the lower half. Water is sucked up one or more siphon tubes, dropped into the box hanging outside the aquarium, and passed through the charcoal and the floss before returning to the tank. One siphon tube must reach almost to the bottom to pick up any settled wastes. The siphon tube should have a pinched or screened end so that fish are not sucked up.

Compared to the corner filter, this type is easier to clean, does not take up space inside the tank, and is not likely to lose particles of floss inside.

UNDERGRAVEL OR SUBSTRATA FILTERS come in a variety of models. These are highly desirable filters, consisting of plates that fit on entire floor of tank and are covered by one or two inches of gravel. Water and debris are sucked through the gravel. Oxygen-loving bacteria that grow on the plate decompose the debris, reducing it to a harmless silt that stays under the plate. This cleans and somewhat purifies the water. A disposable charcoal cartridge fits where bubbles are released.

Be sure not to use fine gravel in the filter. It will sift through slits of plastic plates of filter.

THE AIR PUMP is the companion of the filter. It is located above the water level, outside the tank. Aquarium tubing connects the filter to the pump. Between them there should be an oil and dust filter that prevents back pressure into the pump. Air travels through the tubing to the filter. Outside filters may come with their own magnetic-drive motors and not need pumps.

Many types of pumps are available. Before buying a pump, check to make certain it can handle the gallon volume of your tank. Remember that the pump will be working 24 hours a day. It is wiser to invest in a high-quality pump, which should have a guarantee for a minimum of a year. A good pump will outlast several of the inexpensive ones.

A METHOD OF FILTRATION for tanks of more than 25 gallons involves a combination of outside and undergravel filters. This eliminates the charcoal cartridge on the undergravel post. Siphon out about a fourth of the water every month and replace with fresh. Before pouring gravel over the filter, cover bottom of tank with an inch of water and shake the submerged plate to remove air bubbles. Cover filter with gravel and sweep your fingers through it to release air pockets.

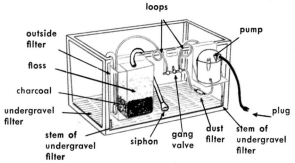

Gravel

fine (sand)

medium

best gravel for sub-strata filter is irregular in shape and about ¼ inch in size

coarse

GRAVEL

Put the tank in its permanent location before adding gravel or water. The tank cannot be moved after these are added. Use natural gravel. This is the usual and familiar floor covering for most freshwater fish. Colored gravels are attractive but are not recommended because they may fade or cloud the water.

Buy sterilized, washed aquarium gravel without lime or metals. As a precaution, wash the gravel again. Use a clean plastic, glass, or enamel container. A newly purchased plastic pail is just right for aquarium use. Rinse gravel in hot tapwater. Continue to rinse until the water runs from the pail crystal clear. For good measure, wash the gravel five more times. Finally, rinse the gravel in cold water before pouring it into the tank. Slope the gravel upward toward the back of the tank—from one to two inches. In this way, any debris falling to the bottom will settle in the front where it can be seen and easily siphoned or netted. Sloping also gives depth and interest to the aquarium.

Aged tapwater is usually best. Allow the water to aerate for several days in the tank. This will age or season it. Tapwater is generally treated with chlorine, which irritates a fish's gills. If the gills are badly damaged, they may be unable to assimilate enough oxygen, and the fish will die. Fortunately, chlorine and a few other harmful gases will escape the water during the aging period. Mineral compounds, however, will increase in concentration as water evaporates. Many aquarists keep a supply of aged water stored for use in emergencies.

TO FILL A TANK, allow the water to dribble slowly down the front pane of glass. Do not dump in all the water at once. Fill the tank halfway, then add the decorations (p.16). Then add water to within one or two inches of the top.

UNFIT WATERS for use in an aquarium:

Rainwater, which is often contaminated with atmospheric poisons.

Lake or stream water that may be poisonous or harbor harmful bacteria and parasites.

Demineralized water, because it lacks the essential minerals fish need.

Water that has been stored in iron, zinc, copper, or lead vessels is poisonous to fish.

Yellowish water in established tanks indicates overcrowding and overfeeding. To remedy, siphon the tank partially and replace with fresh water; add new charcoal to the filters.

Cloudy water the first day after setting up a new tank is probably due to bacteria. Never introduce fish into such water. If the water is not crystal clear in two weeks, remove water and start over.

In an old tank, cloudy water may be due to a filter not functioning properly. It is most often caused by a dense growth of microorganisms that are decomposing debris in the tank. Make certain the fish are not fed too much and that they are not overcrowded. Less than a gallon of water per inch of fish is crowding. Cloudiness of this sort cannot be removed by ordinary filters, though a diatom filter will do so. Siphon off half the water; eliminate the excess food and/or fish. Add new water and then check to see if problem has been remedied.

GREEN WATER is caused by blooms of microscopic plants (algae). The algae are not harmful but are not attractive in large amounts. If all of the algae die and decay, they foul the water, utilizing the oxygen needed by the fish. If the water has become opaque, make a complete change of water and clean the gravel. If the water is just beginning to turn green, the excessive growth of algae can be discouraged by reducing the amount of light. Algae-eating fish can be introduced and also larger plants that will compete with the algae for nutrients in the water.

pH kit

DH kit

FETID WATER is generally a sign of decay. An odor is a danger signal. Find its source and eliminate it.

CONCENTRATION OF HYDROGEN IONS, called pH, indicates whether the water is acid, neutral, or alkaline. Hard water is alkaline; soft water is neutral to acid. Knowing the pH of the water is especially important when breeding fish.

A sudden change of pH implies that something is wrong in the tank, such as overcrowding or overfeeding. Slight daily fluctuations are normal.

Kits are available for measuring and setting the pH. Do not change to the desired pH quickly. Wait several hours for water to stabilize to get new, accurate reading. Activated carbon keeps water neutral. Resin charcoals buffer the water to a specific pH.

DH, degree of hardness, increases due to calcium and magnesium compounds, possibly from dead snail shells or some kinds of ornaments. Excessively hard—150 ppm or more—can be softened by diluting it with distilled water (no more than 60 percent).

CIRCULATION OF WATER is important to the aquarium inhabitants. Bubbles from filters do not add oxygen to the water. The oxygen is absorbed at the surface, then circulated through the tank.

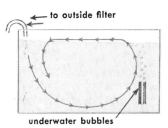

to outside filter

underwater bubbles

DECORATIONS

A balanced aquarium—containing only fish, water, gravel, and plants—is a challenging project for the advanced or experienced hobbyist. For beginners, the result is often dead, decaying plants that mess up the tank.

Plants are important in the theoretically balanced aquarium. As they grow, they utilize the wastes from the fish, but because the water is circulated by a pump and filter, the amount of oxygen supplied by the plants becomes insignificant. If the fish are fed greens, the live plants can be eliminated from an aquarium without harm.

Artificial aquarium plants look authentic and are long-lasting. Check for exposed wires that may rust and contaminate the water. If possible, buy plants that are constructed entirely of non-toxic plastic, such as polyethylene.

A creative arrangement of live plants or a mixture of live and artificial plants is pleasing and also provides fish with food and with a place to spawn. The aquarium plants themselves are a growing hobby, with more than 150 species from which to select. Aquascaping involves blending colors, shades, texture, and size. Larger, fast-growing plants are anchored at the back of the tank; smaller ones at the sides, center, and front. Rocks can be blended with the plants to achieve a natural-looking underwater world. Just make certain to leave space for the fish to swim. Digging or plant-eating fish can ruin an aquascape in only a few hours. In addition, fish medications such as methylene blue or salt (more than 1 teaspoon per gallon) can kill plants.

Plants are sold rooted, bunched, or floating. Buy only crisp plants, with no brown, dead parts. Keep them moist until you get them to your aquarium. Avoid using planting sticks; fingers are best. Plants need 8 to 10 hours of light daily.

ROOTED PLANTS are often most beautiful. Locate each plant by digging a wide, shallow hole in the gravel. Hold the plant by its top and fan out the roots in the hole before refilling it. Anchor the plant if necessary. The swollen base of the stem should be just above the surface of the gravel. Cut the light in half a few days to allow plant to root.

The plants obtain nourishment from the gravel, so in older tanks place the plants where the gravel has been fertilized by the fish. Rooted plants grow well in tanks with undergravel filters, but the roots become tangled in the filter plate. When the tank is dismantled for cleaning, the plants may be injured, resulting in their stunting or death. Clip off old, brown leaves.

MADAGASCAR LACE PLANTS are expensive and hard to keep alive. Live plants are propagated from bulbs planted just under the gravel. The tough, brittle leaves grow slowly but may become 2½ feet long. Rub off algae or dirt that may collect on the leaves. A midwinter drop of 10 degrees is beneficial for this plant but not for delicate fish. The plant is used best as a somewhat isolated centerpiece. It requires at least 10 hours of subdued light per day.

MADAGASCAR LACE PLANT
Aponogeton fenestralis
to 2½ ft.

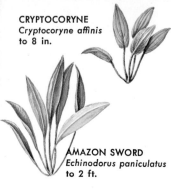

CRYPTOCORYNE
Cryptocoryne affinis
to 8 in.

AMAZON SWORD
Echinodorus paniculatus
to 2 ft.

PIGMY AMAZON SWORD
E. tenellus
to 4 in.

**HAIR GRASS OR
NEEDLE GRASS**
Eleocharis acicularis
to 1 ft.

HYGROPHILA
Hygrophila polysperma
leaves to 2 in.

**CAPE FEAR
SPATTERDOCK**
Nuphar sagittifolia
leaves to 9 in.

CRYPTOCORYNE does well without great amounts of bright light, as in tanks with floating plants. Slightly acid, soft aged water is best. Many species are available. Some plants produce red leaves that grow above the surface of the water.

AMAZON SWORD, a typical rooted plant, grows new plants by sending out runners. These should be pushed below the gravel. Amazons are an effective decor. As soon as young plants develop roots, they can be snipped from runners and transplanted.

The Pigmy Amazon (to 4 in.) will carpet a 10-gallon tank. The regular Amazon (to 24 in.) should have at least 25 gallons in which to spread. One plant may have as many as 40 leaves. In new tank setups with hard water, Amazons are delicate. If the leaves discolor, increase the daily light duration.

HAIR GRASS grows in thickets 6 to 12 inches high. It spreads by runners. Hair Grass has only stems, no leaves. It survives in warm or cool water.

HYGROPHILA is a rooted plant that does best when planted in small bunches. In good light, it grows well. Hygrophila may be propagated either by cuttings or by leaves.

CAPE FEAR SPATTERDOCK grows 6 to 8 inches tall, in slightly acid water with plenty of light. But only plants that have a good root system.

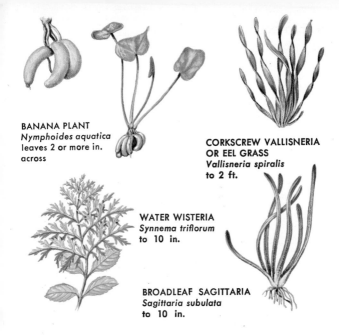

BANANA PLANT
Nymphoides aquatica
leaves 2 or more in.
across

**CORKSCREW VALLISNERIA
OR EEL GRASS**
Vallisneria spiralis
to 2 ft.

WATER WISTERIA
Synnema triflorum
to 10 in.

BROADLEAF SAGITTARIA
Sagittaria subulata
to 10 in.

BANANA PLANT produces banana shaped tuberous roots that lie on top of the gravel. A few stems grow from the roots, with leaves unfolding as the stems approach the surface. Plant-eating fish like to eat both the stems and the leaves. For this plant, native to ponds and slow waters of southeastern U. S., the water temperature should be 70 to 82 degrees F.

WATER WISTERIA grows to 10 inches tall in slightly acid water. It requires little light. The bright green leaves may grow right out of the aquarium.

CORKSCREW VALLISNERIA, a popular aquarium plant, is a tape-leafed grass that forms a dense underwater forest in either warm or cool water. Note the dark green stripe that runs down the middle of each leaf. The leaves will grow to the surface of a tank of practically any size.

SAGITTARIA thrives in warm or cool water. It resembles *Vallisneria* but differs in having a striped leaf. Some species are as short as 2 inches; others grow much taller. All do best in fertile gravel in hard water.

19

BUNCHED PLANTS are more popular than either rooted or floating plants. They are propagated from cuttings, many of them later producing roots. Remove the band securing the bunch and snip off the bottom tips of the stems. Strip the leaves from the lower inch of the stem and anchor them in bunches of two to four stems on top of the gravel. They will grow fast and need trimming regularly. Use the upper cutting—the top, growing part of the plant—and throw away the bottom part. In new water, add an aquarium plant vitamin and mineral supplement, available at pet shops.

CABOMBA, its fine leaves arranged in a fan-shape pattern, requires water cooler than 72 degrees F. Without sufficient light and aeration, it falls apart and sheds its leaves over the bottom. Goldfish can nibble it down to stubs.

A sudden change in water conditions will also kill this sensitive plant. Locate it at the back of the tank, for healthy plants grow quickly—to a length of three feet. Several species of *Cabomba* are stocked in most pet shops.

ELODEA, or Anacharis, is a hardy, popular plant that does not demand critical water conditions. (*E. callitrichoides* does require water at 72 to 85 degrees F.) Fish may nibble on it, but generally it grows fast enough to replenish itself and may add an inch or more to its length daily. Locate it at the back of the tank, and prune the foliage often.

BACOPA has thick, fleshy leaves, spaced far apart on the stem. It is a slow grower and needs at least 10 hours of light daily. Floating does not show off this plant at its best.

HORNWORT is fragile and crumbles easily. In nature, it floats just below the surface in cold water. In an aquarium it can be anchored. A few pieces provide refuge for baby fish. Hornwort does not develop **roots.**

WILLOWMOSS is a cold-water plant, doing well in water below 72 degrees F. The water should be well aged. If anchored with a porous rock, it will attach to surface.

AMBULIA, its leaves in swirls around the stems, grows fast in soft water. It needs 8 to 10 hours of light daily. Remove it routinely and rinse in fresh water. This results in bushy plants.

ELODEA OR ANACHARIS
Elodea densa
(also *Egeria densa*)
to 10 ft. long

CABOMBA OR FANWORT
Cabomba caroliniana
3 or 4 ft. long

E. callitrichoides
to 10 ft. long

BACOPA
Bacopa caroliniana

HORNWORT
Ceratophyllum demersum

WILLOWMOSS
Fontinalis gracilis

AMBULIA
Limnophila sessiliflora
leaf whorls 3-4 in. across

LUDWIGIA
Ludwigia natans
leaves to 1½ in. long

DWARF FOUR-LEAFED CLOVER
Marsilea hirsuta

MILFOIL OR FOXTAIL
Myriophyllum spicatum

LUDWIGIA survives at most water temperatures in aquariums, from cool to warm. At lower temperatures—60 to 70 degrees F.—the underside of the leaves of the species illustrated turn a pretty red. Some of the leaves are adapted for growth above the surface (emersible), others far below the surface (submersible).

Given adequate space, these plants become quite bushy. They produce yellow flowers. New plants are started from cuttings planted in soil fertilized with fish wastes. Several species of this bog plant are available in pet shops.

DWARF FOUR-LEAFED CLOVER is a small, hardy plant that does well at most temperatures. It is showy, hence attractive when planted at the front of the aquarium. The leaves are on long stems.

MILFOIL turns light green and becomes brittle in inadequate light. If it receives 8 hours of light per day, it is fast-growing and turns a deep, bright green. Several species of Milfoil are available in shops. They prefer cool waters and are easily choked by the debris stirred up by rooting fish. Compare Milfoil with Cabomba, Hornwort, and Ambulia and note the differences.

FLOATING PLANTS reduce the amount of light that can enter the water, hence are desirable where it is important to have a dimly lit tank. It is wise to grow them in patches so that some light can reach the plants below. If the aquarium has just been set up, add some aquarium-plant vitamins to the water. Floating plants are generally relished by herbivorous fish.

WATER SPRITE is a floating plant sold in bunches. Even if anchored in the gravel, it will stretch its leaves to the surface and produce new plants that multiply as they float. Water Sprite does well in most aquariums, as its demands are not critical.

DUCKWEED is very popular for shading an aquarium from strong light. Large fish especially like to eat Duckweed, which can quickly cover the whole surface of a tank with its tiny leaves. In large tanks or in outside pools, it may become a nuisance.

NITELLA has no roots. The water should be neutral to alkaline. Most fish eat *Nitella*, and they also seem to enjoy swimming around it.

CRYSTALWORT grows fast. It requires a minimum of six hours of light daily. Keep it thinned to an inch in thickness. Fish spawn in this plant.

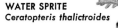

WATER SPRITE
Ceratopteris thalictroides

DUCKWEED
Lemna minor
leaves about ½ in. across

CRYSTALWORT OR RICCIA
Riccia fluitans

NITELLA
Nitella gracilis

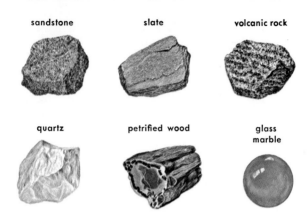

| sandstone | slate | volcanic rock |
| quartz | petrified wood | glass marble |

Some Safe Aquarium Ornaments

ORNAMENTS are second on the list of decorations. Thousands of plastic or ceramic decorations can be bought, ranging from miniature sunken ships to divers and treasure chests. Most of them are safe, though unnatural. Avoid using seashells and corals, for unless properly treated, they can poison the water. Coins are also dangerous.

Neighborhood rocks may be the best. They can be used to create natural-looking caves, arches, houses, and mountains. Children enjoy helping with these creations. All stones are not safe, of course. Soft rocks, such as cement or limestone, make the water alkaline as they dissolve. Rocks containing metals will poison fish. If you are in doubt, ask the advice of a geology instructor. Remember, too, that ornaments subtract from the volume of water, so take them into account when stocking the tank or adding medications to the water.

To prevent fish from leaping out, aquariums should have a lid that stretches all the way across the top. A pane of glass may be used, but do not place it directly on the aquarium frame. Leave about a fourth of an inch of air space by putting a small rock under the glass at each corner.

If the tank is away from windows, as it should be (p. 8), the room's light is not adequate for the growth of most plants. An aquarium reflector hood is generally used to provide overhead lighting. Fluorescent lights cost more initially than do incandescent lights, but they use less electricity and last longer. Further, they do not heat up, while incandescent lights (normal filament bulbs) can overheat small tanks. Be sure to purchase tubes that are made especially for aquarium reflectors. Do not buy bulbs in hardware stores. Those that are made to produce natural light for the tank are best. Too much light causes green algae to grow abundantly. Most plants need 8 to 10 hours of light per day.

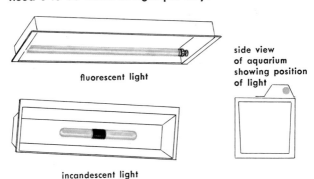

fluorescent light

side view
of aquarium
showing position
of light

incandescent light

TEMPERATURE

Goldfish and some other kinds of aquarium fish do not require water warmer than room temperature. If tropicals are the choice, however, an aquarium heater is necessary. These heaters are equipped with thermostats so that the water is kept at a constant temperature. When the heater is operating, a small light bulb glows. To set the unit, heat the water to the correct temperature, then turn the adjustment knob until the light blinks. Plug in the heater only when it is properly submerged. Before siphoning, unplug the heater.

A heater will melt plastic, so secure it well away from the sides of a plastic tank. Large fish, like cichlids, will bump heaters and break them. Their tanks must be equipped with the unbreakable type of heater that is now on the market.

The temperature of the water should be checked daily with a thermometer. Because the temperature is critical for many tropicals, it is wise to buy an inexpensive second thermometer so that the accuracy of one can be checked against the other.

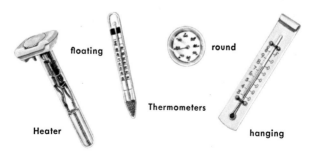

floating

round

Thermometers

Heater

hanging

SHOPPING LIST

This shopping list will help in estimating the total cost of your aquarium setup. Write down the price beside each item. Using this list should also eliminate the need for extra trips to the store to pick up forgotten items. To this list you can finally add the fish and their assortment of foods, which should be purchased about two weeks later.

fish net

plant weight

feeding ring with suction cup

aquarium and stand
filter
charcoal and floss
air-line tubing
valves (if needed)
dust and oil filter
air pump
gravel
pH kit
water hardness testing kit (optional)
plants and weights
ornaments
reflector
light bulbs
heater
thermometer
siphon
pail and sponge
feeding ring
fish net
emergency tonic (p. 30)

algae sponge

valve

pail

BASIC DIET

An aquarium animal's well-being depends not only on the quality of its environment but also on the food it eats.

VARYING THE DIET is important for any animal. Few foods contain all the essentials of a balanced diet, and so do not feed the same food more than a few times consecutively, even if the fish obviously like it.

Many commercial and live foods are available, and hundreds of types of packaged foods can be found on store shelves. Choose those with the highest percentages of proteins, fats, minerals, and vitamins. Today there is no excuse for not having a variety of foods —even as many as a dozen.

OVERFEEDING is the most common mistake of beginners. Feed fish frequently, at least two times daily, but feed small amounts. Make certain that absolutely all of the food is consumed at each feeding—say, within ten minutes. Leftover food fouls and spoils the water. Unless the bottom feeders begin to eat it, this food should be removed by siphoning. Never shake a container of food over the water unless the flow can be controlled perfectly. Sprinkle pinches of food over the surface.

FEED FISH A VARIETY OF FOODS.

LIVE FOODS

Daphnia

white worm

brine shrimp

tubifex worms

mosquito larvae

gnat larvae

baby livebearer

IN THE KITCHEN are many foods that are fine for fish. Shredded canned spinach is a good vegetable supplement. Fine baby cereals are also excellent. Lean beef heart or liver and fish or shrimp can be shredded to the proper consistency. For baby or tiny fish, wrap a small piece of hard-boiled egg yolk in wet linen. Squeeze one or two drops through the linen into the tank. Pieces of food should be no greater than half the size of the fish's mouth.

FEEDING BABY FISH may be an inconvenience but is rewarding. Many can be raised on commercial baby foods, but they grow slowly. The growth of newly hatched fish is speeded by feeding them infusoria—a broth of microscopic plants and animals. Most pet shops carry infusoria. An alternate is using the egg yolk already described above.

Older fry are fed newly hatched brine shrimp. Eggs of brine shrimp and directions for hatching them can be bought at the pet shop.

ADULT FISH are usually fed at least twice daily. One meal consists of a high-quality staple food. The other can be one of the following:
live tubifex worms
thawed sea lettuce
shrimp meal
meal pellets
baby guppies or mollies
vegetable flakes and
    tablet foods
conditioner daily food
live brine shrimp
commercial liquid tube
    food
shredded white fish
canned spinach or cereal food
chopped or shredded
    beef heart
chopped earthworms

Live foods are now frozen or freeze-dried for convenient feeding. They can be substituted occasionally for the real thing. Thaw frozen foods to room temperature; do not refreeze.

If you go on vacation, put a "vacation feeder" into the tank. Healthy fish can survive for more than a week without food. If friends volunteer to feed your fish, caution them not to overfeed.

29

Only healthy fish should be purchased, and their good health should be maintained. It is important to be able to recognize a healthy fish's appearance. Know the anatomy and behavior of the various species kept. Study the diagram and also the charts on pp. 34-35. Check each pet once every day for any changes that may indicate an illness.

Even in the best cared-for aquarium, problems may appear suddenly. Sick fish must be treated immediately. A day's delay may mean the death of the fish. Keep on hand some good emergency general tonics to treat the most common fish disorders. Ask a reliable dealer to assist you in selecting these broad-spectrum medicines, of which there are many.

IN HEALTHY FISH, the fins stand straight out. They are not frayed or held close to the body. Select active fish that have clear eyes, bright colors, and a smooth skin and no discolorations. Distended or red gills indicate infection. Do not pick the fish that lingers shyly behind decorations when others of the same species are in clear view begging to be fed. Even such shy types as Gouramis are alert and dash about madly when disturbed.

NEVER TAP on the aquarium glass when window shopping for fish. Tapping confuses and frightens the fish, causing them to dash into objects and injuring themselves. Vibrations can also result in internal disorders.

The advice commonly given not to buy from a tank containing even one dead fish is misleading. The dealer may have gone through all of his aquariums scooping out many dead fish just ten minutes before you walked into his store. Those remaining may be ill. One or two dead fish in a tank does not necessarily mean that all of the inhabitants are ill. If the dead fish have clearly visible signs of disease, the water may be contaminated. If a dead fish looks as though it was healthy and other fish in the aquarium are nibbling at its body, chances are that it died of old age or perhaps as a result of shipping. During their long journey from their source (p. 35), fish may be bruised or go into shock.

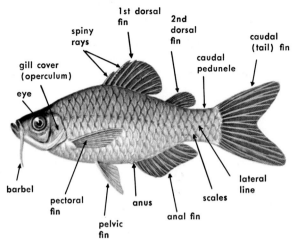

Labels on figure:
- 1st dorsal fin
- spiny rays
- 2nd dorsal fin
- caudal (tail) fin
- caudal pedunele
- gill cover (operculum)
- eye
- barbel
- pectoral fin
- pelvic fin
- anus
- anal fin
- scales
- lateral line

PARTS OF FISH (idealized)

BEFORE MAKING SELECTIONS give the dealer a list of the kinds of fish you have.

The dealer should be gentle with the fish as he catches them so that they are not harmed or unnecessarily frightened. If a fish jumps and lands on the floor, wet your hands before picking it up. Dry hands will rub off some of the fish's protective slime and leave it susceptible to disease.

The water in which the fish travel from the shop to your home must be taken from the tank in which they were living. If the fish you select are from six tanks, then you should have at least six containers. Too many fish in one results in nipped fins, especially if aggressive species are mixed with shy.

The net used for catching the fish should be clean. If the dealer does not have a separate net for each tank, have it dipped in a disinfecting solution, such as salt or methylene blue, to remove any harmful microorganisms. This disinfecting should be done between each catch.

USE PLASTIC BAGS for shipping fish. Make certain that plenty of air is trapped above the water in each bag, which should look like a blown-up balloon. Do not allow the salesman to fill the bag by breathing into it. His respired air is full of carbon dioxide, and the fish may suffocate before they reach their destination. The air should come either from an air tank or from the room.

WITH THE PLASTIC BAG IN POSSESSION, make one last check for signs of disease before taking the fish from the store. Be careful not to jiggle the bag. Do not allow young children to carry it, for they may drop or sway the captives and harm them. As soon as possible, place the plastic bag in a brown paper bag. The darkness will help calm the frightened creatures. Hurry home. Remember, the fish have a limited amount of oxygen.

AT HOME, float the plastic bag(s) in the seasoned aquarium to equalize the temperatures of the two waters and also to allow the fish to become acquainted with their new surroundings. After fifteen minutes, open the bags and slowly (over a period of about ten minutes) dip water from the tank into the bags. After the bags contain mostly aquarium water, net the fish and free them into their new home. Dispose of the water from which they were just removed. Some aquarists recommend isolating new specimens for a week or two before introducing them into an established community tank. If a spare tank and equipment are available, this is a good precautionary step against introducing a disease.

float bags in aquarium
to equalize temperature

DO NOT WORRY ABOUT CATCHING A DISEASE from pet fish. The few diseases that are transmittable to man are rare and can be contracted only by eating the infected fish.

PREVENTIVE CARE is easier than treating diseases. Take extra time to keep the tank clean, at a constant temperature, and the fish well fed. On the same day that fish are purchased, buy some broad-spectrum medicines for treating the most common diseases.

SALT AND DYES used in treating fish diseases may kill plants. Isolate diseased fish in a plantless aquarium or use alternative medicines, such as antibiotics.

AQUARIUM PESTS are:

Diatoms, which form a brown coating on glass, gravel, and decor. They are often incorrectly called brown algae. An infestation can be killed by increasing the amount of light.

Algae can be dangerous (p. 15) in large amounts. Both green and blue-green algae may coat glass, gravel, and decorations. To eliminate them, reduce the amount of light and/or introduce kinds of fish that eat algae.

Hydras may form a white coating on the glass. They are carnivorous, hence a threat to fry. Gouramis eat them.

Dugesia or *Planaria* are free-living flatworms that are found in many freshwaters. In an aquarium, they eat fish eggs and fry. Bettas eat them.

NO TREATMENTS are recommended in the disease section of the health chart (pp. 34-35). For each illness there is also a large selection of cures.

Diagnosis of the disease is most important. After determining the ailment, go immediately to the local pet store and buy the medicine that claims to be effective in treating it. Read and follow the directions on the package.

Before buying the medicine, describe the symptoms to the fish specialist in the store to make certain your diagnosis is correct. If in doubt, consult books that have detailed accounts and prescriptions. External symptoms of diseases often overlap. For any disease, microscopic examination is the final diagnosis.

DRUGS that are commonly used to treat the various kinds of diseases of aquarium fish are:

Antibiotics — erythromycin, chloramphenicol (chloromycetin), chlorotetracycline (auteomycin), oxytetracycline (terramycin), penicillin, streptomysin, and tetracycline.

Dyes — acriflavine, brilliant green, malachite green, and methylene blue.

Others — castor oil, copper, formalin (37-40% formaldehyde), mapacrine hydrochloride (mepacine), merbromin (mercurochrome), picric acid, potassium dichromate, potassium permanganate, quinine hydrochloride (quinine), silver nitrate, and sodium chloride (common salt).

HEALTH CHART

DISORDERS	SYMPTOMS	TREATMENTS
Inherited		
Tumors	growths on body, especially tail	no cure known
Deformities	usually in spine	no cure known
Environmental (often leading to secondary infections):		
Constipation (from improper diet; not enough exercise)	appetite dwindles; belly swells slightly; feces may trail	feed flake food saturated with castor oil, or shreds of earthworms; vary diet
Stomach or Intestinal (from monotonous diet)	sluggish; belly area usually dark or light	starve fish for several days, then feed varied diet
Shock (due to changes in water temperature or chemistry)	loss of color and appetite: may gasp, fins held close	heat water to 80-85 degrees F.; add 2 tsp. sea salt per gallon
Swim Bladder Disease (a temperature shock)	gasp at surface and gulp air	as above
Suffocation (from overheating, overcrowding, decay)	gasp at surface	eliminate cause
Chlorine Shock (form of suffocation)	same as above	age water before use
Torn Fins, Wounds	fins split or frayed, scales missing	warm water to 80 degrees F.; give salt treatment and a balanced diet
Deformities	abnormal spine or fin development	from improper diet; may be inherited

DISEASES	SYMPTOMS
Viral Diseases	
Cauliflower Disease, Lymphocystis (a pox virus)	cauliflower-shaped growths may be white, gray, red
Bacterial Diseases	
Columnaris, Body Fungus, Mouth Fungus (Chondrococcus)	not a fungus; fins degenerate, split; white patches turn slimy; fish may shimmy; contagious
Fin-rot, Tail-rot, Black Molly Disease, Fin Congestion (from invasion of bacteria)	fins are red and streaked with veins; may degenerate

Bacterial Gill Disease	fish ride around in currents of water; sluggish; loss of appetite; gills become inflamed
Pop-eye, Exophthalmus	eye(s) bulge; may be clouded
Dropsy (Pseudomonas, Aeromonas)	fish swells; scales may stand out; fish lies on bottom; eyes may protrude; ulcers
Tuberculosis (Myxobacterium)	loss of weight, appetite, color; ulcers, eyes may protrude; loss of equilibrium; yellow spots on caudal peduncle
Furunculosis (Aeromonas)	open ulcers, mainly dorsal

Fungal Diseases

Fungus (Saprolegnia)	white or gray blotches, usually on wounded areas or weak fish; contagious and common
Eye Fungus	as above but in eye
Ich, White Spot (Ichthyophthirius)	white flecks, spreading from fins; common and contagious

Protozoan Diseases

Velvet, Rust (Oodinium)	yellow or rust-colored patches
Slimy Skin Disease (caused by Chilodonella, Cyclochaeta, Costia, Trichodina), and others	color lost; white, gray, bluish-white or off-white slime excreted from skin and covers body
Neon Tetra Disease (Plistophora)	color fades; equilibrium is lost; affects other species
Whirling Disease (Myxosoma)	same symptoms as above
Discus Disease	looks like tiny worms on head

Helminth Diseases

Skin and Gill Flukes (Gyrodactylus)	fish dash about, rub against objects; exhaustion; contagious
Gill Flukes (Dactylogyrus)	same as above but restricted to gills, which become inflamed; fish have difficulty breathing; flex gill covers frequently
Leeches (Piscicola)	heart-shaped grayish worms
Black Spot Disease (Diplostomiasis, Neodiplostomum)	brown to black cysts cover body; carried by snails
Eye Cataract (Hemistomum)	eyes get cloudy

Crustacean Diseases

Anchor Worm (Lernaea)	common on Goldfish; fish rub on gravel and objects
Fish "Louse" (Argulus)	attaches externally; dark brown to pale green

SOURCES OF TROPICAL FISH

Every year millions of fish are shipped to markets from breeding houses and fish farms. As soon as the baby fish reach a size suitable for selling, they are packed in large, heavy-gauge plastic bags filled with water and oxygen. These are placed in cardboard cartons, insulated with styrofoam and hurried to their destinations by truck or by airplane.

The fish descriptions in this book refer to the native ranges of the species. Most of the fish bought in stores probably came from commercial breeding houses or fish farms. Fish that are not prolific in captivity, however, are best collected in the wild. Rapid air transport has greatly reduced the risk of getting these fish to markets. It has also made it possible to introduce new, unusual species. This is especially appealing to the hobbyist and makes it worthwhile to hire natives to net fish in the wild.

CONDITION TANK BEFORE BUYING FISH

A balanced aquarium (p. 16) containing no filtration is difficult to achieve. The aquarium must first be conditioned—that is, it must support beneficial nitrifying bacteria that remove from the water toxic compounds, such as ammonia, and convert them into less toxic substances, such as nitrites, nitrates, nitrous oxide, and free nitrogen.

The aquarium will not be successful unless this nitrogen cycle is operating properly. It can do so at an optimum in an under-gravel filter bed (p. 11) and will start about two weeks after the new tank is set up.

No delicate animals should be placed in the aquarium until the cycle or conditioning begins. The stabilization can be hastened by adding some gravel or water from an established aquarium or by introducing some hardy animals during the first two weeks while the cycle is getting underway toward attaining a balance.

Snails were once considered to be the best scavengers for an aquarium. Today, algae-eating fish and catfish are used in tropical aquariums because of the disadvantages of snails. Even with no special food or care, one snail can in a short time produce numerous offspring. Soon there are literally hundreds of snails. Though they do consume uneaten foods, they also contribute their own wastes, and they also eat fish eggs. Wild or pool-bred snails may carry dangerous fish diseases. Despite these negative features, snails can add interest to the aquarium. They help keep the glass and decorations clean.

MYSTERY SNAILS are desirable and not prolific. They need an abundance of food. They will not harm aquatic plants if given an occasional lettuce leaf or some cooked spinach.

RAMSHORN SNAILS, very popular for either warm or cold water aquariums, are bright red. Fish eat hatchlings.

WANDERING SNAIL should be avoided. It eats plants and produces a poison fatal to fish.

MALAYAN BURROWING SNAIL plows in search of food, preventing gravel from packing. Water should not drop below 70 degrees F.

ACUTE BLADDER SNAILS are exceptionally prolific in most aquariums—to the point of being considered pests. Fish cannot eat the hard-shelled babies.

MYSTERY SNAILS
Ampullaria
to 2½ in.

BLADDER SNAIL
Physa acuta
to ½ in.

WANDERING SNAIL
Lymnaea ovata peregra
to 1 in.

RAMSHORN SNAIL
Planorbis corneus
to 1¼ in.

MALAYAN SNAIL
Melanoides tuberculata
to 1 in.

AFRICAN AQUATIC FROG lives its entire life under water. It will not hop out of the tank. Needs varied diet of fish foods, both dry and live. Arrange the aquarium as for any tropical fish, using floating plants. This animal is used in laboratories for pregnancy tests.

SALAMANDERS and newts need damp land areas, for they leave the water occasionally. They eat fish eggs, insects, worms, snails, and unwary small fishes. These amphibians are quiet and quite tame, accepting food from fingers.

SMALL TADPOLES are safe to add to an aquarium. They eat infusoria. As adults, however, they will eat fish if they can catch them. Most frogs must get out of the water to bask and will jump out of tanks. In established tanks, they can also stir up a mess as they kick.

FRESHWATER GHOST SHRIMP are not true shrimp. In the wild, they eat algae and debris. Captive specimens will eat most fish foods. Their home is on the tank's floor, but they will not uproot or eat plants. Large fish will gobble them up.

TADPOLE
(many kinds
are suitable)

AFRICAN AQUATIC FROG
Xenopus laeuis

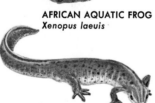

JAPANESE NEWT
OR SALAMANDER
Molge pyrrhogastra

FRESHWATER
GHOST SHRIMP
Gammarus spp.

BABY TURTLES are probably the most mistreated pets sold in pet shops and variety stores because their needs are so poorly understood. If treated well, they may live for more than ten years.

DO NOT put them in shallow, plastic "turtle bowls." In these bowls, they are too cramped, and the water fouls quickly. Do not feed them commercial turtle foods or raw hamburger. Commercial foods are usually dried ant eggs and flies, offer little or no nutrition. The raw hamburger contains too much fat, which bloats the turtles.

PUT THE TURTLE in an aquarium in which the water is deep enough for it to exercise. Hang turtle rafts, available in pet stores, several inches below the reflector lights. Allow the turtle about 8 hours of light each day for basking. If the water is not heated, leave a light on all night on cool evenings. The water temperature should be 72 to 80 degrees F.

Feed the turtle a balanced diet; fish foods, dog food, lean beef, raw fish, cottage cheese, raw shrimp, freshwater snails, worms, fruits, hard-boiled eggs, and lettuce. A turtle will eat better if it is in company with other turtles. If fed daily, it will not bother fish, though the long, flowing fins of a slow-moving fish may be too much to resist.

Turtles become unbelievably tame. They will swim to fingers to grab morsels of food.

Given basking lights and a proper diet, they rarely become ill. Swollen eyes or soft shells are a result of mistreatment. For swollen eyes, place the turtle in an antibiotic or sulpha bath two times daily. Feed it as much as it will eat of its favorite foods. Soft shells are hardened by giving the turtle large amounts of sunshine and calcium supplements in the diet. The cruel practice of painting shells will eventually kill the poor victims.

AROWANA
Osteoglossum bicirrhosum
to 20 in.

TROPICAL FISH FAMILIES

BONY-TONGUED FISHES (Osteoglossidae)

This family of freshwater fishes, belonging to the same order as herrings, is distributed over South America, Southeast Asia, Borneo, Sumatra, Australia, and Africa. All of the members are large.

AROWANAS are sometimes imported from South America as juveniles, only 3 to 4 inches long. If you are willing to provide for a fish that will grow to 20 inches long in captivity, the Arowana makes an unusual pet that may live more than ten years. Their relationship to prehistoric fish makes them especially interesting and unusual aquarium pets.

Young specimens are peaceful; older ones must be isolated. Plan ahead. A tank of at least 75 to 100 gallons will be needed when the youngster grows up. In a roomy tank the species shows off its graceful, sleek movements. Temperature of the water should be 75 to 78 degrees F. Arowanas prefer large live foods, such as Goldfish, but they can be taught to take chunks of raw fish or beef. Parents are said to carry their eggs and babies in their mouth.

FRESHWATER BUTTERFLYFISH (Pantodontidae)

This family contains only one genus and one species, occurring in western Africa.

FRESHWATER BUTTERFLYFISH is a leaper. Spreading its large pectoral fins, it can glide over the surface of the water. If the lid is left off an aquarium, this fish is likely to "fly" out.

Note the large, upturned mouth. This is a feature characteristic of fish that live in the upper strata and feed at the surface.

The tank should be spacious (20 gallons or more), dimly lit, and moderately planted, especially with a few floating plants. The water should be slightly acid, soft, and 75 to 85 degrees F. Feed these fish by sprinkling food on the surface. Chunks of raw beef or fish, flying insects, earthworms, mealworms, and live fish are relished. Because they are carnivorous, Butterflyfish should be kept only with their own species.

FRESHWATER BUTTERFLYFISH
Pantodon bucholzi
to 5 in.

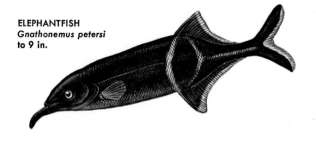

ELEPHANTFISH
Gnathonemus petersi
to 9 in.

ELEPHANTFISH (Mormyridae)

ELEPHANTFISH, native to the warm, freshwaters of tropical Africa, are not bred commercially but are occasionally imported for sale in pet shops. Though they are expensive, their oddity makes them of interest. One of the several species is illustrated here.

An Elephantfish may show playful behavior. With its surprisingly flexible, long nose, it will dig and feel around in search of food. It generally ignores prepared dry foods, hence live foods must be provided. Because of its small mouth, an Elephantfish can swallow only small bits.

House the Elephantfish in a large tank with aged water at a temperature of 75 to 80 degrees F., in a normal pH and with some plants. Since the fish is nocturnal, provide dark areas in which it can hide. Because of its shy, delicate nature and its occasional aggressive behavior, the Elephantfish is not a good community fish and is not recommended for amateur aquarists.

CHARACINS (Characidae)

Characins, found in South and Central America and in Africa, comprise one of the largest families of freshwater aquarium fishes. Most of them have an adipose fin and teeth. All lack barbels.

Characins scatter eggs throughout the tank; they are not live-bearers. With few exceptions, they do not care for either the eggs or the offspring. The small schooling, or shoaling, species are among the most popular aquarium fish because of their color, peaceful temperament, hardiness, and ease of handling. Members of the family usually do best in semi-lit aquariums with soft, slightly acid water.

BLIND CAVEFISH, natives of caves in the region of San Luis Potosi, Mexico, have such highly developed senses of smell and touch that they rarely bump into anything. They swim with their head tilted slightly downward, eating any food contacted. Blind Cavefish scavenge, but provide a varied diet of foods that will sink to the bottom. Though suitable community fish while young, adults may become aggressive. The water temperature in the aquarium may range from 70 to 85 degrees F.

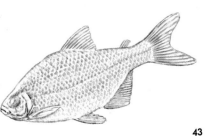

BLIND CAVEFISH
Anoptichthys jordani
to 3 in.

BLOODFINS show off their brilliant red fins best when they are in large schools in a roomy tank. They lay non-adhesive eggs and will eat them if they are not removed after spawning. For this species, the optimum water temperature is 75 degrees F., but temperatures. from as low as 65 and to as high as 85 tolerated.

CARDINAL TETRAS are believed by many aquarists to compare in brilliance with the saltwater tropicals. They resemble the smaller Neon Tetra (p. 52), but in this species, the red extends down the ventral side of the body. Cardinals are less common, hence more expensive than Neons.

SPLASH TETRAS display a courtship behavior unlike any other characins. After much playing and chasing, the male leads his female to the spawning place he has chosen. This is located about two inches above the surface of the water. In nature, the pair may spawn on an overhanging leaf or a rock. In captivity, a small pane of sanded glass angled across the aquarium will suffice. The glass must be sanded so that the eggs will adhere.

The pair first jump out of the water and cling to the surface a number of times without spawning. After these preliminary jumps, the actual spawning jumps are made, with eggs deposited and fertilized in small groups. About 50 to 175 eggs are laid over a period of an hour or so. As many as a dozen leaps are made in this time.

The female then swims away and shows no more interest in the eggs, but the male returns periodically and splashes water on the eggs with his

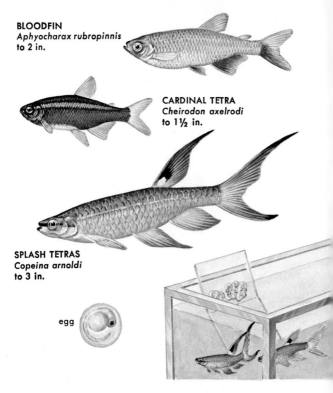

BLOODFIN
Aphyocharax rubropinnis
to 2 in.

CARDINAL TETRA
Cheirodon axelrodi
to 1½ in.

SPLASH TETRAS
Copeina arnoldi
to 3 in.

egg

tail. This prevents them from dehydrating. The eggs hatch in three days, and the young either fall or are splashed into the water. Hatchlings should be separated from the parents.

Splash Tetras do best in neutral water at 75 degrees. F. Cover the tank so that the fish do not jump out. "Ripe" females—that is, filled with eggs—are plumper and shorter than the males.

SWORDTAIL CHARACINS, native to Trinidad and Venezuela, should be purchased when they are mature, because they are then less susceptible to disease. A mature male has a threadlike extension from the gill plate and at the end of the extension a shovel-like appendage called a "corynopoma." During courtship, the male shows off this extraordinary feature to his partner. Older males also have extended rays in the ventral fins.

In mating, a capsule, or spermatophore, is deposited in the female's oviduct. Inside this capsule are sperm that can live for an extended period of time. They can fertilize eggs expelled by the female long after the male is removed.

Because these fish are not obsessed with eating their eggs or young, they are easier to raise than are most. Swordtail Characins do well in pairs and are quite peaceful in a community tank, with the water maintained at 70 to 80 degrees F. and with plants. They should be fed a varied diet.

BLACK TETRAS, from Paraguay, are peaceful when young but may become aggressive with age, nipping other less active, less aggressive fish. By the time the fish mature, the black fades to a light gray. Color fading also occurs in younger fish when they become ill or are frightened.

Females are noticeably distended when ripe. Provide plenty of space for these active egg scatterers in water that is 72 to 85 degrees F. Schools of these fish can move with amazing speed to snatch up bits of food in their varied diet. They require the same care as other tetras (p. 48). Longfinned Black Tetras, a new strain, are gaining in popularity.

SWORDTAIL CHARACIN
Corynopoma riisei
to 3 in.

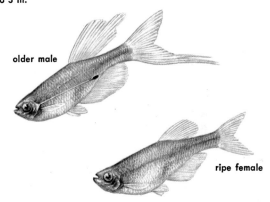

older male

ripe female

**LONGFINNED
BLACK TETRA**
(a variety of
the Black Tetra)

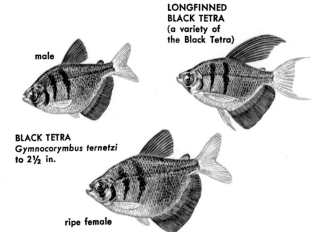

male

BLACK TETRA
Gymnocorymbus ternetzi
to 2½ in.

ripe female

GOLDEN TETRAS have an intense gold shine, difficult to show in an illustration. Requirements for Golden Tetras, a peaceful schooling species from British Guiana, are the same as for other tetras. They do best in groups of four to eight kept in large, roomy tanks in which they can school. A natural environment is provided by dense clusters of plants placed at random. Both bright (sunny) and dark (caves) areas should be available. The water should be slightly acid, soft and low in lime. Optimum temperatures range from 70 to 80 degrees F. Give them a varied diet.

All of the tetras are from South and Central America. Members of the genus *Hemigrammus* have scales at the base of the caudal fin. Most members of the genus *Hyphessobrycon* do not.

SILVERTIP TETRA, a peaceful shoaler from southeastern Brazil, looks handsome against a dark background, with overhead lighting to emphasize its silver-tipped fins. A red strain is also available.

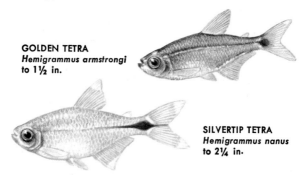

GOLDEN TETRA
Hemigrammus armstrongi
to 1½ in.

SILVERTIP TETRA
Hemigrammus nanus
to 2¼ in.

BUENOS AIRES TETRA, from the La Plata Basin around Buenos Aires, grows to 4 inches long, hence should be kept in a large tank. This species is frequently housed in schools while young, but older fish may nip the fins of any fish kept in the tank with them. Females in particular become quite aggressive. The temperature of the water should range from 68 to 78 degrees F. Plant the tank sparingly, for this tetra likes to nibble on plants and uproot them. It has a good appetite and will gobble large pieces of food. Feedings should be frequent.

GLOWLIGHT is a mid-strata swimmer that looks very impressive in large schools in an aquarium with a dark bottom and sprinkled with plants. Its beauty approaches that of the Cardinal Tetra (p. 44). In spawning, the partners lock fins and roll from side to side in thickets of plants. Optimum water temperature is 75 to 80 degrees F. The Glowlight should be fed the basic diet. This species is sensitive to Neon Tetra Disease (p. 35).

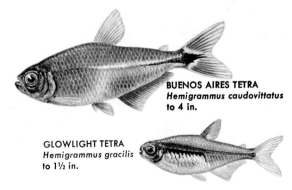

BUENOS AIRES TETRA
Hemigrammus caudovittatus
to 4 in.

GLOWLIGHT TETRA
Hemigrammus gracilis
to 1½ in.

HEAD AND TAIL LIGHT, also called Beacon, occurs throughout the Guianas, especially in the Amazon region. A peaceful community fish, it likes a wide variety of foods. It is a shoaling fish, a mid-strata swimmer, and needs plants in which to retire. The water should be soft and slightly acid, kept at 75 to 80 degrees F. Because of its iridescence, this fish lives well in the company of Neons, Cardinals, Glowlights, and other such shoalers. The ripe female is more plump than the male. Males sometimes have a small white spot on the anal fin. They develop a hooked anal fin that can easily snag in a net.

RUMMYNOSE, from the lower Amazon, is gaining in popularity. In proper conditions, which are a dimly lit tank and soft water at 78 to 80 degrees F., the red nose, single dark horizontal line, and black striped tail stand out magnificently. This species does best in schools.

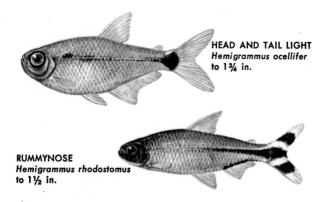

HEAD AND TAIL LIGHT
Hemigrammus ocellifer
to 1¾ in.

RUMMYNOSE
Hemigrammus rhodostomus
to 1½ in.

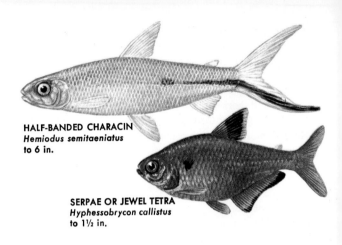

HALF-BANDED CHARACIN
Hemiodus semitaeniatus
to 6 in.

SERPAE OR JEWEL TETRA
Hyphessobrycon callistus
to 1½ in.

SERPAE OR JEWEL TETRA is variable in its colors. Studied extensively, this species is divided into six subspecies by some authorities. Most of them have a red tint over their body. Some have a black spot on the shoulder region. Serpaes school from the middle to the lower strata. The water should be soft, neutral, and 70 to 80 degrees F. Feed them the standard varied diet. They may nip fins.

HALF-BANDED CHARACINS are rarely found in aquaria because they do not breed successfully in captivity. If obtained, however, this species is peaceful in a community tank of at least 20 gallons. The schools will hover in the lower strata, but they are capable of rapid movements, jumping out of the tank and skillfully dodging or leaping from nets. Keep them in neutral water at about 75 degrees F. and feed them a basic diet, including plants on which they can nibble.

FLAME TETRA is also called Red Tet from Rio, the Rio referring to Rio de Janeiro where this species is believed to have originated. The Flame Tetra likes an aquarium with plenty of hiding places, because it is easily frightened and will lose its brilliant colors during such sessions. It is a peaceful shoaler, or schooling fish, requiring neutral water at 70 to 75 degrees F.

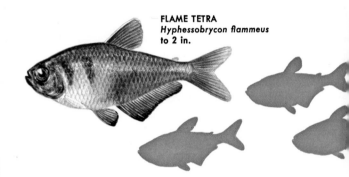

FLAME TETRA
Hyphessobrycon flammeus
to 2 in.

NEON TETRAS come from the Peruvian Amazon where they live in shaded jungle waters. Neons should therefore be housed in a semi-dark aquarium with the bottom and sides in dark colors. Black tissue can be taped to the sides of the aquarium to simulate the natural environment, but keep the tissue at least half an inch from the water level at the top of the tank because the dye in the paper can kill fish. Light the aquarium dimly from above. If necessary, use patches of a floating plant to reduce the intensity of the light.

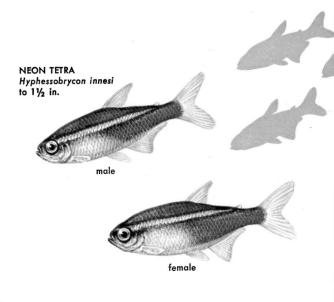

NEON TETRA
Hyphessobrycon innesi
to 1½ in.

male

female

In the Neon's jungle habitat, the water is replenished frequently by soft, fresh rain. To provide comparable conditions in the aquarium, add boiled rain water or tap water weekly, maintaining its temperature at 72 to 78 degrees F. and its pH at 6.5. Viewed from above, a ripe female Neon is broader than the male. She is an egg-scatterer.

Neons are shoalers, the schools swimming in the middle to lower strata. The fish is peaceful with others of the same size. Feed a varied diet. Neons are susceptible to Neon Tetra Disease (p. 35).

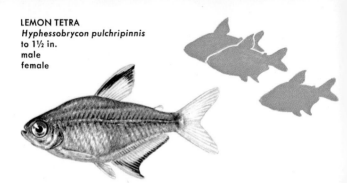

LEMON TETRA
Hyphessobrycon pulchripinnis
to 1½ in.
male
female

LEMON TETRA has a lemon-colored belly, seldom seen in aquarium fish. In a tank, a school of Lemon Tetras looks especially striking with a school of Black Tetras. The Lemon Tetra is a calm but active community fish that needs a bit more care than do most tetras. It is highly sensitive to changes in the pH, temperature, and hardness of the water. If these are abrupt, the fish may go into shock, losing its color or even dying. Water changes must be made gradually, watching the fish carefully to make certain they are not reacting unfavorably.

ROSY TETRA, from the Amazon Basin, is colorful when young but fades with age. Some authorities consider the Rosy Tetra to be a subspecies of the Serpae Tetra (p. 51), different only in having a black spot on its shoulder. Adult males have long, almost hooked dorsal fins. Be careful not to break these fins when handling the males with a net. The temperature of the water should be 72 to 82 degrees F. Vary the diet.

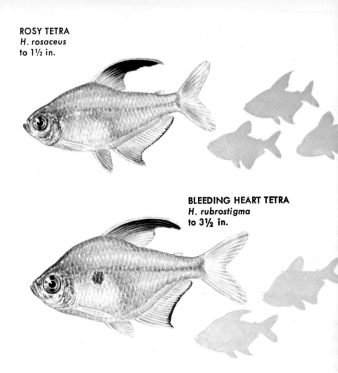

ROSY TETRA
H. rosaceus
to 1½ in.

BLEEDING HEART TETRA
H. rubrostigma
to 3½ in.

BLEEDING HEART TETRA is a larger, more aggressive species than most members of the genus. Keep it in schools of four to ten fish. The tank should be supplied with soft, slightly acid water at 72 to 78 degrees F. Place dense clusters of plants at random throughout the tank to provide a natural environment of both bright and shady areas. Be careful in handling mature males, which have sickle-shaped dorsal fins. Young are sensitive to water changes.

SILVER DOLLARS have a ferocious appearance which, coupled with their large size, could give the impression that this species is undesirable for a community tank. Actually, Silver Dollars are shy. They will not bother fish larger than 1 to 2 inches. Mix them with other species in the beginning, or they will become possessive of their territory and nip the fins of intruders.

Silver Dollars will feed on spinach, fruits, lettuce, and aquatic plants in addition to their daily varied diet. They seem to enjoy uprooting plants, hence it is best to decorate with rocks and artificial plants. Shoals of two to five fish will dash from one hiding place to another in the lower strata. The water temperature should range from 75 to 85 degrees F. With age, Silver Dollars lose any dark spots or stripes.

RED HOOK METS not only live in harmony with the Silver Dollar but also have identical requirements. In size and shape, they are similar to the Silver Dollar, but their bright red anal fin is sickle-shaped. They have not been bred in great numbers in captivity and are rarely seen in aquariums.

EMPEROR TETRAS are beautiful fish that are quite suitable for a community tank with fish of the same size. Males are identified by their extended caudal fin and by their splendid coloration, which becomes especially vivid when they are courting the females. A pair of Emperor Tetras does best in a spacious tank, but since their growth is slow, it may be best to keep them temporarily in limited-size areas. Feed them a varied diet. The optimum temperature for these fish is 72 to 78 degrees F.

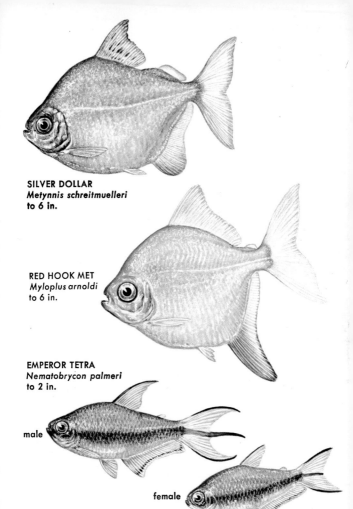

SILVER DOLLAR
Metynnis schreitmuelleri
to 6 in.

RED HOOK MET
Myloplus arnoldi
to 6 in.

EMPEROR TETRA
Nematobrycon palmeri
to 2 in.

male

female

PIRANHAS always create interest, for everyone seems to have heard tales about how schools of these South American fish skeletonize even the largest of victims in a matter of minutes by slicing out large bites with their razor-sharp teeth. Owners who tire of watching their Piranha tear apart other fish for dinner sometimes set them free in the nearest pond, lake, or canal. In the wild, the Piranha becomes a threat to native species, and authorities are justifiably concerned in warmer states that it might become established. For this reason, a permit may be required to keep this fish in your state. Check with state officials before you obtain a specimen. Piranhas are not advised pets for most hobbyists.

Piranhas travel in schools in the wild, but in confinement, they may turn on their own kind. In one instance, two Piranhas of the same species lived in the same tank peacefully for more than a year and a half. Then one morning the head and gills of one of them were found floating on the surface. Keep only one Piranha in a tank!

Provide a Piranha with a place to hide and feel secure, for oddly, this fish will eat only when it senses no danger. Try feeding chunks of non-fatty beef, such as heart, kidney, and livers. Raw fish is sometimes accepted. If the pet does not consume dead matter, try living earthworms, mealworms, tubifex worms, or goldfish (a favorite). Keep the water temperature at about 78 degrees F.

When catching a Piranha, remember that it can easily bite holes in nets and fingers. It may be indifferent to human flesh and not attack hands submerged in the tank for a weekly cleaning but this practice is not recommended.

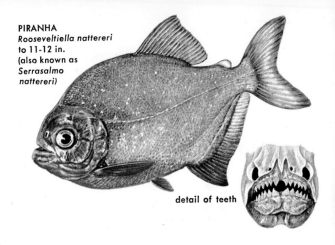

PIRANHA
Rooseveltiella nattereri
to 11-12 in.
(also known as
*Serrasalmo
nattereri*)

detail of teeth

PENGUINFISH are named for their black-and-white markings and for their characteristic tail-down resting position. Although delicate during shipping, these fish become quite hardy after they are established in an aquarium. A school of Penguinfish adds character to the mid-strata of a large tank. House them with fish of the same size or larger, for Penguinfish have a tendency to pick on the smaller fellows. The water should be soft, slightly acid, and 72 to 78 degrees F. The aquarium should include plants for nibbling. Penguinfish will seldom bottom-feed.

PENGUINFISH
Thayeria obliqua
to 3 in.

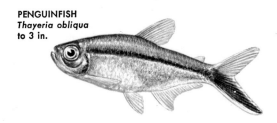

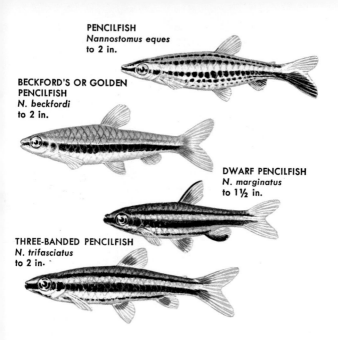

PENCILFISH
Nannostomus eques
to 2 in.

BECKFORD'S OR GOLDEN
PENCILFISH
N. beckfordi
to 2 in.

DWARF PENCILFISH
N. marginatus
to 1½ in.

THREE-BANDED PENCILFISH
N. trifasciatus
to 2 in.

PENCILFISH are native to South America, where they inhabit quiet freshwater streams and lakes. For keeping these fish, the aquarium water should be aged and its temperature maintained at 72 to 78 degrees F. The aquarium should be well supplied with plants.

These torpedo-shaped fish swim in spurts. Some species rest in a head-up position, others in a horizontal position. At night the stripes on their sides fade into indistinct blotches. Do not mix the different species in the same aquarium, for they may become quarrelsome. Keep each species separate and in groups of three or more.

NORMAN'S HEADSTANDER, from the lower Amazon region, lives up to its name by resting and swimming in a characteristic 45-degree head-down position. It dwells in the lower strata of the tank and will isolate itself in a territory which it increases in size as it establishes itself and grows larger. Smaller, less aggressive neighbors will be chased from this territory. This headstander is a jumper, so the tank must be covered. The best water temperature is 75 to 85 degrees F. Watch at feeding time to make certain enough food is eaten from the varied diet provided. Vegetable matter is relished.

SPOTTED HEADSTANDERS are among the most delicate and shy of the aquarium tropicals. Care must be taken to make certain they get enough food. Smaller bits of food are preferred to larger chunks. Aged water and plenty of rooted plants are necessary for success with these fish, and the temperature of the water should be maintained between 72 and 82 degrees F. In groups of two to four, the contrasting black-and-white checkered pattern of the large scales is displayed quite effectively.

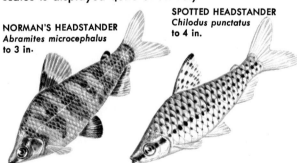

SPOTTED HEADSTANDER
Chilodus punctatus
to 4 in.

NORMAN'S HEADSTANDER
Abramites microcephalus
to 3 in.

RED OR STRIPED HEADSTANDER is one of a special group of characins that inhabit fresh waters of Central and South America and Africa. Because of their interesting shape and striking markings, they are favorites of aquarists. Their name comes from their peculiar habit of resting and also swimming in a head-down position.

The Red Headstander positions its pencil-shaped body, with its three dark brown or black stripes, head down in the water when relaxed. It thrives best in groups of two to four and is peaceful if kept with other fish of the same size. Since it is fond of vegetation, encourage the growth of algae by keeping the tank well lit. Lettuce, spinach, and water plants may be substituted for algae. Augment the diet with other foods.

Note the position of the Red Headstander's mouth which is directed upward like a surface-feeder's. This affects the eating behavior, for when the fish feeds on the bottom, it must invert itself.

LEPORINUS eats vegetation, so provision its tank sparsely with vertical plants on which it will nibble. It will also graze in the lower strata, picking up choice morsels or live and dry foods. The vertical stripes along its sides increase in number by dividing in two as the fish grows.

This fish is a jumper, hence the tank must be kept covered. Some individuals may become pesky, nipping to shreds the fins of other species. Schools of both species of handstanders kept in the same aquarium are impressive. The fish are about the same size and are compatible, and the contrast of the horizontal and vertical stripes is striking.

RED OR STRIPED HEADSTANDER
Anostomus anostomus
to 7 in.

LEPORINUS
Leporinus fasciatus
to 6 in.

HATCHETFISH (Gasteropelecidae)

These fish are native to South America, where they live in the upper strata of soft, slightly acid water. If alarmed, the fish will either hide or use their strong winglike pectoral fins to raise themselves halfway out of the water while gliding quickly along the surface. Keep the aquarium covered so that they do not "fly" out of the tank. Hatchetfish need plenty of surface water in a long tank without obstructions. One area of the tank should provide shade-giving plants in which the fish can hide. Without this refuge, a frightened Hatchetfish may fly into the glass and injure itself.

Hatchetfish are peaceful, but they do not live long in captivity. Community tanks are not recommended because these fish are shy and will not get enough food. They do best in groups of from three to six in water at a temperature of 75 to 85 degrees F. Feed them foods that float or remain in the top strata, including plenty of live food. Adult males appear thinner than adult females when viewed from above. These fish are susceptible to the common Ich Disease, described in the chart on p. 35.

MARBLED HATCHETFISH are the most commonly encountered of the hatchetfish. In the shade of a clump of plants, their silver or gold highlights become pearl-like, and the dark irregular streaks along the sides of the body are quite distinct. In an unfavorable environment, the fish become drab and faded-out. This is the most hardy species of the imported hatchets, and it also has a longer life span than do other species in the group.

SILVER HATCHETFISH are not as durable as are the smaller Marbled Hatchets. Some individuals will accept dry fish foods, but many demand live meals. In the wild, they utilize their "flying" ability to catch passing insects. In captivity, they can be fed fruit-flies that are first almost drowned in a jar of water to prevent their escape and then sprinkled on the surface for the fish to pick them up. They will also eat tubifex worms, brine shrimp, and a variety of fish foods. Silver Hatchetfish are known to live more than a year and a half. They should be kept in slightly alkaline water.

MARBLED HATCHETFISH
Carnegiella strigata
to 2¼ in.

SILVER HATCHETFISH
Gastropelecus levis
to 2½ in.

GYMNOTID EELS OR KNIFEFISH (Gymnotidae)

Gymnotid eels, from South and Central America, are closely related to characins (p. 43). African and Asiatic "Knifefish" are similar in appearance but are not related, belonging to the family Notopteridae. Members of both families, cared for in the same way, are nocturnal and are vicious predators. By waving their highly developed elongated anal fin, gymnotid eels can move either backwards or forwards with equal ease.

BANDED KNIFEFISH lack dorsal, pelvic, and caudal fins, and the pectoral fins are small and transparent. The anal fin is prominent and highly developed. The anus is located under the head. Electric organs enable the fish to survive in the muddy, dark waters of its natural habitat. If the tank is darkened, the Banded Knifefish will adjust to eating during the day rather than at night. Feed live meals and chunks of food. Banded Knifefish are cannibalistic, hence it is wise to keep the species isolated. The temperature of the water should be 72 to 85 degrees F. The life span of a well cared-for Banded Knifefish often extends over ten years.

BANDED KNIFEFISH
Gymnotus carapo
to 12 in.

ELECTRIC EEL
Electrophorus electricus
to 7 ft.

ELECTRIC EELS OR KNIFE EELS (Electrophoridae)

Electric eels lack dorsal and ventral fins. They propel themselves with their large anal fin in the same manner as gymnotid eels (p. 66). Their electric organs, studied extensively, are located over about 80 percent of their body. The tissues forming these organs are positioned one behind the other in columns, like the plates in a battery. Electrical impulses, each lasting only a fraction of a second, are discharged in waves that move from one end of the fish to the other. The amount of voltage generated depends on the total number of plates or "electroplasts" in the eel's body. Receptors on the fish's head receive reflected impulses and aid the fish in finding food or in sensing danger.

ELECTRIC EELS, from South America, are not recomended for the private collector. Each eel requires a tank of a hundred gallons or more. Because they lack scales and have a slimy skin, handling them is not easy. Heavy rubber gloves must be worn, for this fish has about 6,000 plates and can generate up to 800 volts. In a large aquarium with a fine-gravel bottom, hiding places, and soft, slightly acid water, the Electric Eel is long-lived. Usually only live food is accepted, but if the fish is hungry, it will eat chunks of raw beef or fish.

CARPS AND MINNOWS (Cyprinidae)

Cyprinids comprise the largest family of freshwater fish. They are native to Asia, Africa, Europe, and North America and have been introduced to Australia and other areas by man.

A typical cyprinid has an elongate, oval to round body. The caudal fin is usually forked, and there is no adipose fin. Scales are absent on the head, but those on the body are distinct and often are silvery. Barbels are frequently present, but they are limited to two pairs. Cyprinids do not have teeth in their jaws; they chew with pharyngeal teeth, which are toothed plates located in their throat.

After being chased by her mate, a ripe female scatters her eggs. The courting male then fertilizes them. If not immediately separated from their spawn, the couple will gobble their eggs. Fertile eggs will hatch in two to four days. Fry can survive on infusoria (p. 29) for one to two weeks. Thereafter they should be fed commercially prepared food for baby fish.

BARBS may or may not possess barbels. The genus is commonly divided into three groups: those with no barbels, those that have two barbels, and those with four barbels. Regardless of their grouping, all barbs are active schooling fish. Sometimes the larger individuals in a school are aggressive toward smaller fish. Barbs prefer a well-lighted aquarium in which there are at least several plants. The water should be well-aerated and kept at 70 to 80 degrees F. Only a few of the most available species in this large genus are treated here.

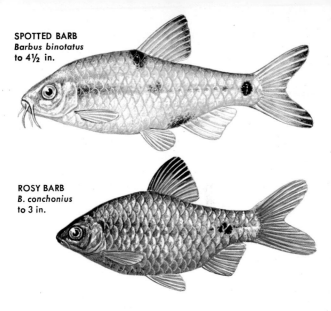

SPOTTED BARB
Barbus binotatus
to 4½ in.

ROSY BARB
B. conchonius
to 3 in.

SPOTTED BARBS are difficult to identify because their spots vary in number, size, intensity, and arrangement depending on the individual's age and origin. For these fish to attain their full or maximum size, a roomy tank with water at 75 to 78 degrees F. and plenty of food are needed.

ROSY BARBS inhabit cool (64 to 74 degrees F.), slow-moving waters of streams in northern India. In their natural habitat, they attain a length of six inches or longer but rarely exceed half this size in an aquarium. Males display a brilliant red or rosy color in the spring spawning season. The female is comparatively drab. Feed these fish the standard basic diet. They live for three to four years.

CUMMING'S BARBS are hardy, active fish from Ceylon. They eat a wide variety of foods and often join scavengers on the bottom to pick up food missed by other fish. Shady spots should be provided in the tank in which the water is kept at 72 to 78 degrees F. In some shipments of this species, the fish display yellowish instead of bright orange fins. Only the males exhibit bright colors.

CLOWN BARBS, among the largest of the barbs, got their name from their color pattern. Two pairs of barbels are evident. This species does best in tanks of more than ten gallons. The water should be 72 to 75 degrees F. and should contain some plants.

STRIPED BARBS are also large, equaling the size of the Clown Barb. Even the young of this species require plenty of space for schooling. Keep the water temperature at 72 to 78 degrees F. These African barbs are sensitive to the conditions of their environment and require more attention than do most species of the genus.

SIX-BANDED BARBS are delicate when young, hence they are often in a weakened condition by the time they reach their destination. Add the recommended dosage of a general tonic (p. 30) before they are introduced to their new home. Feed them an abundance of live foods at first to build up their resistance. The water should be 72 to 78 degrees F., soft, and barely acid. Once established, these shoalers from Sumatra are peaceful community fish. Their beauty increases. Note the six bands, one running through the eye and the last at the base of the tail.

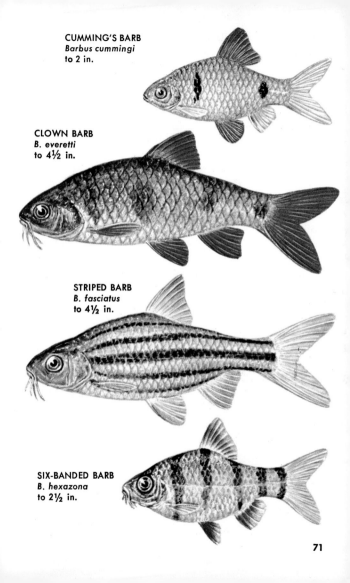

CUMMING'S BARB
Barbus cummingi
to 2 in.

CLOWN BARB
B. everetti
to 4½ in.

STRIPED BARB
B. fasciatus
to 4½ in.

SIX-BANDED BARB
B. hexazona
to 2½ in.

"T" BARBS are called Spanner Barbs by the British. They are native to the Malay Peninsula and Indonesia. Some individuals have red-tinted fins. In young "T" Barbs, vertical and horizontal bars are distinct, but at maturity, these bars are not usually well defined. "T" Barbs are active fish and require space. Schools of two to four fish are ideal for the the larger community aquarium.

BLACK RUBY BARB males in good condition will periodically display their strawberry red bodies and purple head. For most of their life, unfortunately, they show little or no color and resemble the drab females. A majority of males in a tank results in more frequent displays of color but may also give rise to fighting and to nipped fins. Keep this species in water 70 to 80 degrees F., with clumps of floating plants. Black Rubies are susceptible to fungus diseases described on p. 35.

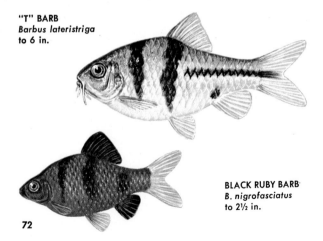

"T" BARB
Barbus lateristriga
to 6 in.

BLACK RUBY BARB
B. nigrofasciatus
to 2½ in.

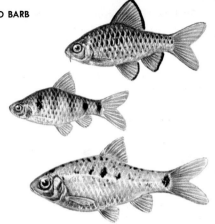

CHECKERBOARD BARB
B. oligolepis
to 2 in.

DWARF BARB
B. phutunio
to 1½ in.

SCHUBERT'S BARB
B. schuberti
to 2½ in.

CHECKERBOARD BARBS are peaceful shoalers that will eat a varied diet and also often graze at the bottom of the tank. A bit of vegetation added to their diet enhances their checkerboard pattern. Keep the lighting subdued and the temperature of the water at 65 to 75 degrees F. These barbs are susceptible to *Oodinium* (p. 35).

DWARF BARBS may be placed in smaller tanks than other barbs, but make certain the water is adequately aerated. Plant the tank sparsely to give the fish schooling space. Maintain the water temperature at 78 to 80 degrees F. Dwarf Barbs are native to India and to Ceylon.

SCHUBERT'S BARBS are not found in the wild. They are a variety developed by a professional breeder and now sold commercially in great numbers. They are hardy, peaceful community fish.

TINFOIL BARBS are among the largest of the barbs. In an aquarium of 30 gallons or more, a young Tinfoil Barb may attain a length of 9 inches in about six months. Tinfoil Barbs are long-lived and active. The older they get, the more colorful they become. The basic diet must be augmented with vegetable matter every day. Avid jumpers, these fish manage to escape by jumping through the smallest crevice in a tank lid. As with most barbs, extremes of temperature result in unhealthy fish that have faded or often little color. Keep the water temperature at 74 to 80 degrees F.

HALF-BANDED OR CHINA BARBS are peaceful, hardy shoalers from China. They will survive in water from 70 to 80 degrees F. Schubert's Barbs (p. 73) were developed from this species.

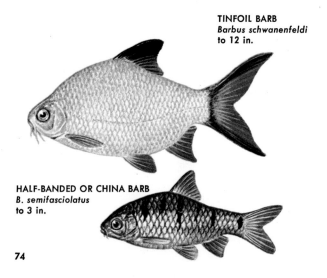

TINFOIL BARB
Barbus schwanenfeldi
to 12 in.

HALF-BANDED OR CHINA BARB
B. semifasciolatus
to 3 in.

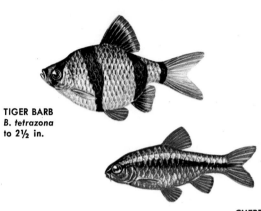

TIGER BARB
B. tetrazona
to 2½ in.

CHERRY BARB
B. titteya
to 2 in.

TIGER OR SUMATRAN BARBS are the most popular of all the barbs for aquariums. They are hardy and retain their color all year. Keep them in large schools. Often one or two of the larger individuals in a school become fin nippers. The only remedy for this is to isolate them. These fish will display their fullest coloring if they are provided with a good basic diet, soft water and plenty of aeration. An albino form is also available.

CHERRY BARBS, from Ceylon, vary in the hues of their striking cherry color. Although hardy, they can also become quite shy if placed with aggressive species. This retiring behavior can be suppressed by keeping them in large schools and allowing only fish of the same size to mingle with them. Keep the water at 75 to 80 degrees F. in a well-planted tank.

GOLDFISH require living conditions different from all other cyprinids described in this book. Not true tropicals, they do best in water at lower temperatures, surviving in conditions that a Neon Tetra, for example, could not. Goldfish can be found in backyard ponds or in pint-size bowls.

A two-inch Goldfish requires at least two gallons of water. In less water, its growth will be stunted and its life span shortened. In a favorable environment, however, a Goldfish will live for as long as 15 years.

If there are too many Goldfish in an aquarium, they will be seen gasping at the surface for air. If the fish must be kept in an unaerated container, select the one that has the largest surface area. More oxygen will be absorbed through this greater area. A bowl with no aeration must be cleaned at least once a week. Even in aerated filtered tanks, Goldfish are messy. There should be only two or three

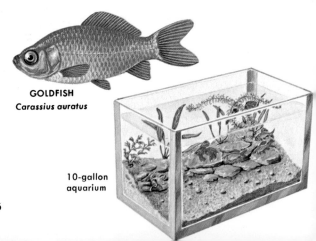

GOLDFISH
Carassius auratus

10-gallon
aquarium

76

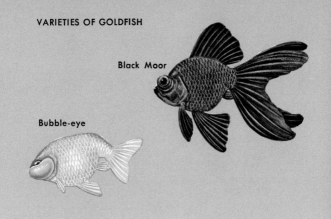

VARIETIES OF GOLDFISH

Black Moor

Bubble-eye

fish per five gallons of water. If only an undergravel filter is used, it will clog rather quickly. A corner filter is better, and an outside filter is still more desirable. An undergravel filter may be utilized in conjunction with either a corner or an outside filter.

Goldfish should always be placed in water that has been aged at least twenty-four hours. Putting them in fresh tapwater may result in a chemical or temperature shock. Clean, uncapped glass juice or milk bottles can be used for aging the water. Goldfish are sensitive to extremes of acid or alkaline water composition. Never use a heater, for Goldfish do best at room temperatures. Water at a temperature above 85 degrees F. will, in fact, encourage infections, especially fungus diseases.

Goldfish that begin to lose their color probably need more vegetation and light. Direct sunlight is best. These fish commonly lose some of their color with age, however.

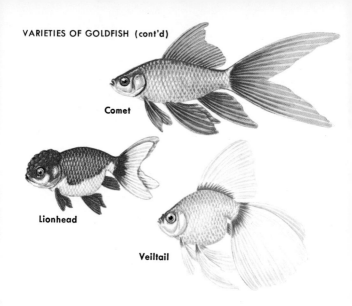

Comet

Lionhead

Veiltail

Allowed to eat their fill, Goldfish will overeat to obesity. Keep in mind that a Goldfish's stomach is normally only slightly larger than its eye. Feed it only enough to fill about "1½ eyes." Goldfish like to nibble on plants, so keep them supplied with a kind they cannot pick to pieces. *Anarchis* is a good plant for Goldfish. Do not feed them exclusively on one kind of boxed food. Follow the basic diet recommended in this book (p. 28).

Goldfish can become territorial. A newcomer placed where others have become established may get all of his fins nipped off or be chased to death. All of the Goldfish that are to co-inhabit each tank should be placed together within one month—before their territories are too firmly established.

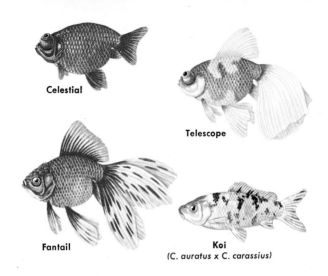

Celestial

Telescope

Fantail

Koi
(C. auratus x C. carassius)

Placed in outside pools, Goldfish do quite well, existing on insects, algae, water plants, or the food you supply them. Unless the water gets too hot or freezes, is polluted, or is in some other way extreme, the fish usually survive. Goldfish thrive singly in aquariums, but outside, they do best in schools.

Despite their great variety of color and form, all Goldfish belong to the same species—*Carassius auratus auratus*. They will grow to a size determined by their environment. In large pools, they may reach a length of two feet.

All of the varieties were developed either by the Chinese or Japanese except the Comet. Its origin is America. Developing new varieties of Goldfish has become a highly specialized field.

DANIOS are a group of active, hardy, undemanding cyprinids. They are slim and streamlined, but ripe females are a bit larger than males and have distended bellies. Danios should be kept in large schools. The optimum water temperature for them is 72 to 80 degrees F.

PEARL DANIOS are native to streams and rivers of Burma. They enjoy sunshine, and in a well-lighted aquarium, they reflect a rainbow of colors from their fins and body. Their pearly sheen may vary from shades of silver to gold, pink, or blue. Keep the tank near a window where it receives sunshine daily, but control the incoming light enough to restrict the growth of algae. The large schools should be predominantly females.

SPOTTED DANIOS are somewhat delicate and do not breed as easily in captivity as do other members of the group. For this reason, they are found only occasionally in stores.

PEARL DANIO
Brachydanio albolineatus
to 2½ in.

SPOTTED DANIO
B. nigrofasciatus
to 1½ in.

ZEBRAFISH
Brachydanio rerio
to 2½ in.

GIANT DANIO
Danio malabaricus
to 4¼ in.

ZEBRAFISH, or Zebra Danio, is boldly striped. Note how the stripes continue down the anal fin. From eastern India, this active shoaler is one of the most popular of the aquarium fish, and because of its abundance, it is inexpensive. Zebrafish may live for two to three years. They are very hardy if kept in schools of about six fish in a roomy tank. Zebrafish are sensitive to sudden changes in the water, but otherwise, they are remarkably tolerant. Keep the temperature of the water at 72 to 80 degrees F., and feed them the basic diet for aquarium fish. During the breeding season, males may acquire a handsome golden sheen. Females lay non-adhesive eggs.

GIANT DANIOS are peaceful, hardy community fish, but because of their size, do not mix them with smaller, mouth-sized species. A large tank, nicely planted, is mandatory. Females lay adhesive eggs.

FLYING FOX
Epalzeorhynchus
kallopterus
to 4 in.

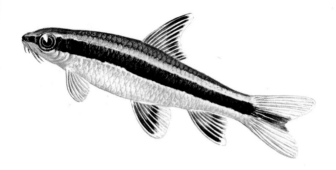

FLYING FOX is also called Trunk Fish because of its strong, protruding snout, which it uses to root food out of the gravel on the bottom. To prevent the fish from bruising its snout, a soft bottom in the aquarium is necessary.

The Flying Fox is omnivorous—that is, it will graze on algae but also readily accepts live foods. It rests on rocks, leaves, or the bottom by supporting its slender body on its pectoral fins. Note the high, curved, dorsal fin.

Because it has not yet been bred commercially and is rarely imported from its native Sumatra, this species is not common in aquariums. One specimen per tank will be peaceful with other species. Two in the same tank will fight each other. The optimum water temperature is 75 degrees F.

FLYING BARBS, from southern Asia, are adapted to life in the upper water strata. Note that the small mouth opening is angled upward, enabling the fish to pick up food from the surface. Flying Barbs also breed at the top of the water. Then, if the water is not shallow, they will dip deeper swiftly to gobble up their own eggs as they sink. Marbles on the bottom of the tank will prevent fish from reaching their eggs and eating them.

In their natural habitat, Flying Barbs swim in small schools, a few individuals often lagging behind to search for food. As their name suggests, these fish are likely to "fly" out of the water. It is therefore important to keep the tank covered. They are hardy and will live for several years in a well-maintained aquarium.

FLYING BARB
Esomus danrica
to 3½ in.

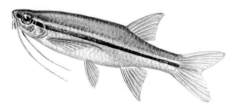

RED-TAILED "SHARKS" are native to Thailand. They have a black, sharklike body with bright orange-red caudal and pectoral fins when they are young and healthy. Their two pairs of barbels and strong lips, with an internal sucking organ, aid them in scooping up their favorite food—algae, which in aquariums should be provided in addition to their basic diet. Soaked green lettuce may be substituted for the algae if necessary. These and other similar "sharks" live in the lower strata, hence they need rocks or caves in which to hide in an aquarium. Keep them in soft, neutral water at a temperature of 72 to 75 degrees F. Individuals may be quarrelsome toward others of the same or different species.

These "sharks" are cyprinids or members of the minnow family and are not related to true sharks, which are cartilaginous fishes.

BLACK "SHARKS" kept in tanks of 100 gallons or more may grow to a length of nearly 20 inches. In smaller aquariums, they rarely exceed 12 inches. They are very hardy and will eat most foods. Algae is an essential for keeping them in good health. Black "Sharks" are aggressive even when young and must be kept with fish of equal size and temperament. Older specimens may be a faded black.

RED-FINNED SHINERS are active minnows that live in streams in midwestern and southern United States. They are members of a large genus of minnows that are hardy and a convenient size for a large home aquarium. Red-finned Shiners require cool (65 to 72 degrees F.), well-aerated water. They will eat most foods offered.

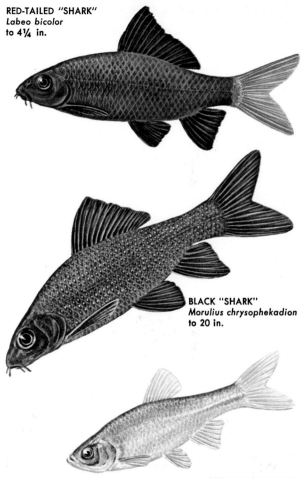

RED-TAILED "SHARK"
Labeo bicolor
to 4¼ in.

BLACK "SHARK"
Morulius chrysophekadion
to 20 in.

RED-FINNED SHINER
Notropis lutrensis
to 3 in.

85

HARLEQUIN RASBORAS, native to the Malay Peninsula, are the most popular of the numerous rasboras available for aquariums. They are peaceful shoalers and become shy if kept with aggressive species. Supply the tank with thickly rooted plants in soft, neutral water at 74 to 80 degrees F. Feed them the basic diet. This species easily becomes infected with Ich disease (p. 35).

SCISSORTAIL RASBORAS have a habit of flexing their forked caudal fins in a scissorlike fashion when resting or when beginning to move. The motion is emphasized by their coloring. This hardy species, needs water of about 72 degrees F. The young fish have an almost transparent body.

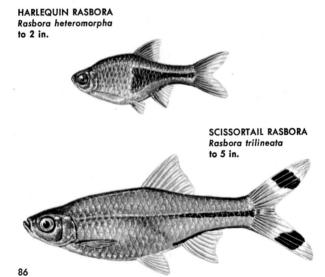

HARLEQUIN RASBORA
Rasbora heteromorpha
to 2 in.

SCISSORTAIL RASBORA
Rasbora trilineata
to 5 in.

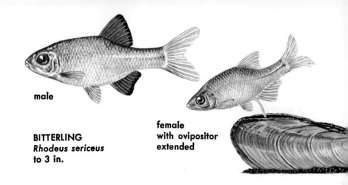

male

female
with ovipositor
extended

BITTERLING
Rhodeus sericeus
to 3 in.

BITTERLINGS do poorly in water above 72 or below 60 degrees F. They are not recommended for tropical fish tanks. They are commonly kept in aquariums in Europe, where they are native, but they are rare in the United States.

Bitterlings and their close relatives in Asia have unique breeding habits. About April, the male changes from silver to red, and the female's ovipositor extends. The male selects a suitable healthy mussel, and his mate inserts her ovipositor into the mussel's incurrent siphon, depositing several eggs. She may repeat this several times over a period of a few days. After each laying, the male saturates the water around the mussel with sperm. Eggs caught in the mussel's gills are fertilized by the milt in the water that is drawn over them. Mussels respire by drawing water into the incurrent siphon, passing it over the gills, then out the excurrent siphon.

The eggs develop and hatch in the gills. After about 30 days, hatchlings have absorbed the food in their yolk sacs. Then they emerge, leaving the mussels unharmed. Both the young and the adults should be fed heavily with live foods.

WHITE CLOUD
Tanichthys albonubes
to 1½ in.

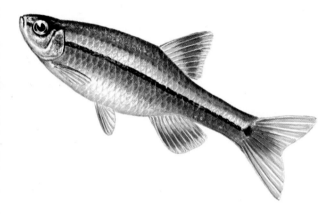

WHITE CLOUDS are hardy cyprinids. The species was discovered in 1932 in a fast-moving stream on White Cloud Mountain near Canton, China. The Chinese Boy Scout who found the fish presented his live catch to his emperor, Lin-Shu-Yen. Biologists later named the new species *Tanichthys* (*tan*, meaning boy, and *ichthys*, fish) *albonubes* (meaning white cloud). White Clouds do best in large schools. They can tolerate a temperature range from 60 to 90 degrees F. but should be kept at as nearly 72 degrees as possible. Mature males have a longer dorsal fin and are slimmer and more colorful than the females. Feed them live food in addition to the basic diet to bring out their richest colors.

GYRINOCHEILIDS (Gyrinocheilidae)

The Algae Eater, from Thailand, is the only popular aquarium fish in the single genus in this family.

ALGAE EATER is a sucking catfish, using its sucking disc in the eating process and also for anchorage in the rapidly flowing water of the streams in which it lives. Most fish breathe by taking water in through their mouth. The Algae Eater takes water in through a slit between the edge and the base of its lips all around its mouth.

Algae Eaters are vegetarians. They are generally kept in aquariums to eat algae off the glass sides and off the decorations. They may also feed as scavengers on the dead bodies of other fish. When young, Algae Eaters are peaceful; older ones may fight each other and also attack any other fish that moves slowly. About one out of five develops this habit. If they release their hold on another fish, a circular red spot is left where the disc was attached. This may become infected. Isolate these undesirable Algae Eaters, or try feeding them more. Increasing the amount of light in the aquarium will encourage the growth of more algae. Keep the water slightly basic and at about 77 degrees F.

ALGAE EATER
Gyrinocheilus aymonieri
to 8 in.

LOACHES (Cobitidae)

Cobitids comprise an Old World family of fish. All of the members have three or more pairs of barbels and no jaw teeth; the fins and scales are small. Cobitids are adapted to life on the bottom; many are burrowers. Some are able to live in oxygen-depleted waters by rising to the surface and gulping air. The intestine is utilized as an accessory respiratory organ. This does not mean that aeration and clean water are unnecessary, however.

Loaches hide during the day. Provide shells, cave-like rocks, or similar sheltering decorations under which they can retire. An extremely domestic pet may abandon its nocturnal habits, but until this departure from the normal is clearly established, it is wise to sprinkle a bit of food in the water before turning out the aquarium lights at night. Loaches have a well-developed sense of smell and can easily find their food in the dark.

KUHLI LOACHES have wormlike bodies and move through the water like snakes. Because of their unusual shape and markings, they are popular aquarium fish. Near the eye is a stiff spine that can puncture the skin, or it may catch in nets. With this spine, the fish can dig in the bottom. Its eyes are protected by a transparent covering. The head is not protected from injury by sharp objects, however, and so it is best to provide a soft bottom, such as sand. If fungus appears on fish's body, treat with triple sulpha. Get advice of fish specialist if growth persists.

Kuhlis do best in groups of at least three. They will crowd together under one rock or ornament. If

KUHLI LOACH
Acanthophthalmus kuhli kuhli
to 3 in.

MYERSI KUHLI
A. myersi
to 3 in.

HALF-BANDED KUHLI
A. semicinctus
to 3 in.

SHELFORD'S PRICKLY EYE KUHLI
A. shelfordi
to 3 in.

SUMATRAN KUHLI LOACH
A. kuhli sumatranus
to 3 in.

this hiding place is lifted, the fish explode in every direction. Keep the temperature of the water at 72 to 76 degrees F. Feed the basic diet.

Note the differences in the five Kuhlis illustrated. All are cared for in the same way.

SKUNK LOACH
Botia horae
to 4 in.

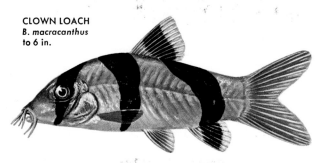

CLOWN LOACH
B. macracanthus
to 6 in.

SKUNK LOACHES, from Thailand, become active at the end of the day. In a brightly lit aquarium, they keep hidden under objects or stay in the shadows. A refuge of their own is recommended. Large curved pieces of cleaned coconut shell have been used successfully. Feed them the basic diet, with plenty of live food and chunks of meat.

CLOWN LOACHES, the most colorful and most popular of the loaches, are imported from Sumatra and Borneo. In display tanks, they often swim peacefully in schools of barbs that are similarly marked and about the same size or slightly larger. Clown Loaches shy from lights at first but usually lose this tendency.

STRIPED LOACH
B. hymenophysa
to 5 in.

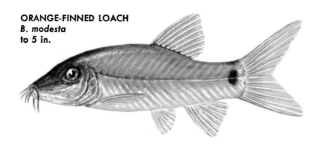

ORANGE-FINNED LOACH
B. modesta
to 5 in.

STRIPED LOACHES are rarely imported. When they are, they sell fast and are expensive. Like other members of their genus, they prefer soft, slightly acid, crystal-clear water at 72 to 75 degrees F. They do well in groups. At night they can be seen darting excitedly up and down and back and forth along the glass. Some individuals become fin nippers.

ORANGE-FINNED LOACHES, only recently available, are sensitive to many tonics, particularly dyes (p. 33). Older individuals are not friendly to most other fish. These fish lack the typical snakelike body of most loaches, but their laterally compressed shape and other body features identify them as cobitids.

SPINY CATFISH (Doradidae)

TALKING CATFISH are seen rarely—both because they are not common and because they hide under the gravel during the day. They come out to search actively for food at night. Provide a soft bottom so that the catfish can bury itself easily.

All of the catfish in this family from South America have bony plates along the lateral lines of their thick body. A spine protrudes from each plate. On the first ray of the dorsal and pectoral fins are stiff spines that can inflict a painful prick. Handle these fish with care! These catfish sometimes emit a croaking sound when captured. They apparently use their modified air bladder to make these noises.

Talking Catfish will attack smaller fish and eat them. They will also scavenge, as do other catfish. Provide them with the basic diet.

TALKING CATFISH
Acanthodoras spinosissimus
to 6 in.

CALLICHTHYID ARMORED CATFISH (Callichthyidae)

Of the armored catfish, *Corydoras* is the predominant genus. The different species in the genus are so similar that they are difficult to identify.

Even the cleanest aquarium can benefit from having at least two peace-loving *Corydoras* that busy themselves most of the time digging in the gravel in search of food. They will not thrive well on just leftovers, however. A varied, balanced diet should be provided, and they are especially fond of live foods. Be sure the food sinks to the bottom, past the fish that are living in the upper strata. Sharp stones will injure the mouths of these probing catfish, so cover the bottom with smooth, rounded gravel.

In their native South America, these catfish live in waters low in oxygen and with muddy bottoms. They have evolved the trait of dashing suddenly to the surface to take in a gulp of air and then hurrying back to the bottom. The air is forced through the intestine, respiration occurring in the heavily vascularized tissues of the hindgut. A proper environment for them consists of water that is neutral, soft, aged, and 65 to 80 degrees F. In clean water, the fish are healthier and also more energetic.

A sharp spine is located on the dorsal fin of many species. Be careful not to snag this spine in nets. Also, a prick from one of these spines is painful, the hurt lasting for an hour or more.

AENEUS CATFISH, also called Bronze Catfish, are the most popular of the *Corydoras*. Older specimens are extremely hardy, ideal for any aquarium. If a larger fish tries to make a meal of one, the catfish's spiked fins snag in the predator's mouth. Usually, the catfish is spit out. Occasionally, a catfish becomes permanently hooked in the attacker's throat. In such cases, both the predator and the prey die.

Adult female Aeneus Catfish are fuller-bodied than the males. A smaller albino variety of this species is often available. The albinos generally purchased are juveniles about half an inch long. Their pink bodies show clearly in most aquaria.

AENEUS CATFISH
Corydoras aeneus
to 3 in.

albino variety
to 2 in.

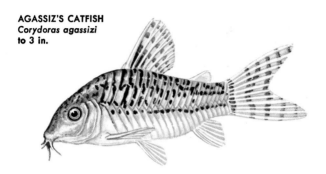

AGASSIZ'S CATFISH
Corydoras agassizi
to 3 in.

AGASSIZ'S CATFISH is small and stout. The fish was named for Louis Agassiz (1807-1873), who was a professor of biology at Harvard University. Agassiz was known for his work with both recent and extinct types of fishes. He believed firmly in studying animals in their natural environment.

Agassiz's Catfish enjoys the company of other catfish of the same genus. Although not typical schooling fish, they may search for food on the bottom in groups, or loose schools. If they are not overcrowded and are well fed, all of the different species of *Corydoras* are peaceful.

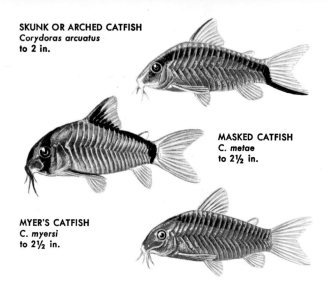

SKUNK OR ARCHED CATFISH
Corydoras arcuatus
to 2 in.

MASKED CATFISH
C. metae
to 2½ in.

MYER'S CATFISH
C. myersi
to 2½ in.

SKUNK CATFISH, MASKED CATFISH, MYER'S CATFISH

—these three species confuse amateurs attempting to identify their pets. Further, retailers may label them incorrectly. Their differences are shown clearly in the illustrations above, however. All three are cared for identically.

A pair of *Corydoras* of the same species and sometimes of different species soon become intimate friends in an aquarium. One always checks to see if the other is in sight. As one example of their desire for companionship, only one Skunk Catfish was kept in a community tank for about six months. Then another was added to the aquarium. It was greeted with great enthusiasm by the original catfish. All day it circled the newcomer excitedly and was thereafter always at the side of its companion.

ELEGANT CATFISH are not really as elegant as many other *Corydoras*. In fact, they are rather plain. Interestingly, the two identifying, irregular, dark bands on each side may fade or darken according to the fish's mood. Unlike most catfish in this genus, this species may leave the lower water strata to search above for food on plants and rocks.

ELEGANT CATFISH
C. elegans
to 2½ in.

DWARF CATFISH
C. hastatus
to 1½ in.

DWARF CATFISH are ideal for the five-gallon fish tank. Because of their small size, they are not cramped in these smaller quarters. Be sure to keep at least two in each tank.

Dwarf Catfish leave the bottom strata in small groups to frolic in the mid-strata. Other fish that are extremely aggressive may pick on these small catfish, so keep them with mild-mannered fish.

LEOPARD CATFISH are strikingly spotted, hence their name. Try pressing a small square of dry, frozen tubifex worms against the front pane of glass inside, about half an inch above the gravel. At the same time, supply any other fish with enough to keep them occupied above. You will discover that all or nearly all members of the *Corydoras* community join in the feast.

SADDLEBACK CATFISH, like all of the *Corydoras*, have an outer "armor" that helps prevent many external diseases. Every other occupant in a tank may be inflicted with Ich (p. 35), but the catfish will remain healthy. They are not totally immune to disease, however, and once sick, they seem to be more difficult to cure than most other fish.

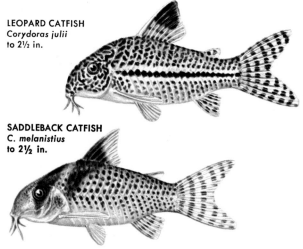

LEOPARD CATFISH
Corydoras julii
to 2½ in.

SADDLEBACK CATFISH
C. melanistius
to 2½ in.

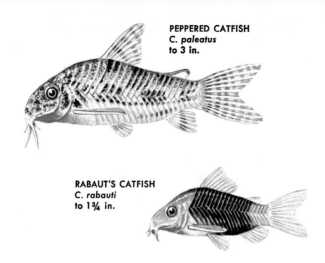

PEPPERED CATFISH
C. paleatus
to 3 in.

RABAUT'S CATFISH
C. rabauti
to 1¾ in.

PEPPERED CATFISH have a sprinkling of small, dark spots over their body. Before breeding, males swim excitedly around in one area. A male and a female then pair off. With their mouths, they clean any possible spawning sites. During spawning, the two join—breast to breast. The female lays eggs in a pocket formed with her ventral fins, and there they are fertilized by sperm ejected by the male. The female then sticks the eggs to clean surfaces that were previously selected.

RABAUT'S CATFISH is a dwarf species that may be easily snagged in a net. If this happens, turn the net inside-out carefully and submerge it in the water where the catfish is to be placed. If the catfish must be handled, keep in mind that the spines can cause a painful puncture.

SUCKER-MOUTHED ARMORED CATFISH (Loricariidae)

Several diverse forms comprise this family of armored catfish that live in small, swift-flowing streams of northern South America. They use their "sucker" mouths for attaching to or holding onto stationary objects and also for feeding. The "sucking" mouth is subterminal or projected downward for feeding on vegetation on the bottom. As they feed on plants in their natural environment, these catfish also consume many tiny animals. For this reason, the vegetable diet of those in captivity must be supplemented with other foods. In all members of the family, three or more rows of bony scutes or plates extend from the head along the length of the body. Place these fish in tanks of aged water that is richly planted and is 65 to 78 degrees F.

TWIG CATFISH are unfortunately short-lived and shy in captivity. To avoid obtaining a half-starved specimen, purchase only from tanks that have an obvious growth of green algae. If algae are not abundant in your tank, add soft peas or chopped lettuce or spinach (boiled about one minute) to the water regularly until a growth is obtained.

TWIG CATFISH
Farlowella acus
to 6 in.

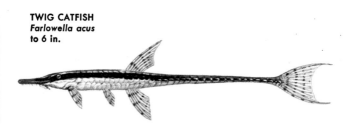

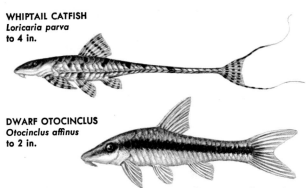

WHIPTAIL CATFISH
Loricaria parva
to 4 in.

DWARF OTOCINCLUS
Otocinclus affinus
to 2 in.

WHIPTAIL CATFISH are easily camouflaged in the gravel on the bottom of an aquarium. Keep their water well aerated and clean. Do not house these fish with messy animals, such as Goldfish, that demand a cleaning of the tank frequently. If it is necessary to do a complete cleaning, save half the water. Submerge any algae-covered rocks or plants so that they do not dry while the aquarium is being cleaned. Do not scrub the sides or bottom of the tank completely clean of algae. After the aquarium is cleaned, leave the lights on longer than usual to encourage a rapid regrowth of the algae and other plants in the tank.

OTOCINCLUS are the smallest common aquarium sucker catfish. They remain small, harmless scavengers and are not destructive—that is, they will not eat plants or dig up the bottom. These little catfish specialize in cleaning algae off plants. Keep them in small groups of at least four. This is a delicate species, and if there is not sufficient vegetable food, it will die quickly.

PLECOSTOMUS CATFISH grow large. They should not be kept in tanks smaller than 25 gallons. Because they become aggressive, only one per tank is recommended. It can be put in a tank with communities of larger fish. Petrified wood is often used in the aquarium's decor because its surface is ideal for supporting mats of soft algae and also because this fish likes to camouflage itself on the "woody" surface while eating or resting. Use water that has been aged at least one month.

These fish are difficult to catch. They will dart from one hiding place to another, and even if cornered against the glass, they will attach themselves to it firmly with their sucker mouth and will not swim into the net. They must be slid along the glass to get them out of the water. Use a soft leaf to break their suction and get them into the net. Once in the net, the catfish commonly snags its high dorsal fin. Be careful not to injure the fish in removing it.

The Bristle-mouthed Catfish is closely related to Plecostomus but is easily distinguished by its prominent "whiskers."

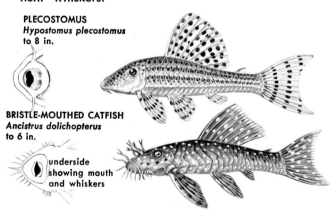

PLECOSTOMUS
Hypostomus plecostomus
to 8 in.

BRISTLE-MOUTHED CATFISH
Ancistrus dolichopterus
to 6 in.

underside
showing mouth
and whiskers

BANJO CATFISH
Bunocephalus coracoideus
to 7 in.

BANJO CATFISH (Bunocephalidae)

BANJO CATFISH are unarmored catfish from South America. Their head is wide and flat. The name of the genus, *Bunocephalus,* means "hilly head," referring to the bumps that extend also down the sides. A soft, sparsely planted bottom is essential because of the fish's digging behavior. Banjo Catfish are nocturnal, so provide plenty of daytime hiding places. They are omnivorous feeders. Keep the temperature of the water at 70 to 75 degrees F.

GLASS CATFISH (Siluridae)

GLASS CATFISH stay in the mid-strata, suspended in small schools. Peaceful and slow-moving, they do poorly if mixed with active species. They snatch their food as it sinks by on its way to the bottom. They relish live foods. Tubifex worms enclosed in sterile gauze or cheesecloth and dangled in the water allows them to feed freely. In appropriate lighting, Glass Catfish reflect rainbows of color.

GLASS CATFISH
Kryptoptereus bicirrhis
to 4 in.

PIMELODID OR ADIPOSE FIN CATFISH (Pimelodidae)

Pimelodid catfish range through southern Mexico, Central America, and South America. All members of the family have a long, slim body. The caudal fin is forked, and the dorsal fin, which has at least one erect spine, is set far forward on the body. The adipose fin is large. Pimelodids usually possess three pairs of barbels that sweep back along the body.

SLENDER CATFISH are nocturnal, which is typical for members of the family. The larger and more cluttered their tank is, the more they enjoy it. Roots, plants, rock piles, and decorations are ideal places for hiding during the day. These catfish do best in water that is neutral, aged, and 70 to 80 degrees F. In older fish, the stripes disappear.

POLKA-DOT CATFISH are particularly fond of worms but will gobble up most meaty foods. They will overeat so much that their stomachs bulge, raising their whole body well above the gravel. If not fed well enough, however, they may attack other fish. Mature specimens lose their spots and become bluishgray. Some young have no spots.

SHOVELNOSE CATFISH are oddities. If you have a spare shallow tank (30 gallons or more), this may be precisely the fish to please you. Note the flattened head and the ducklike snout. The mouth, under the snout, is large enough to engulf chunks of food of considerable size. Give this species the same care as other members of this family.

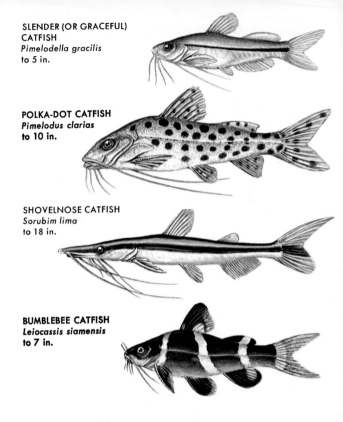

SLENDER (OR GRACEFUL) CATFISH
Pimelodella gracilis
to 5 in.

POLKA-DOT CATFISH
Pimelodus clarias
to 10 in.

SHOVELNOSE CATFISH
Sorubim lima
to 18 in.

BUMBLEBEE CATFISH
Leiocassis siamensis
to 7 in.

BAGRID CATFISH (Bagridae)

BUMBLEBEE CATFISH, from the Old World, are similar to the pimelodids (p. 106), but their skin is naked, with no scales or bony plates. Peaceful and long-lived in a community tank, these catfish will make a meal of a neighbor's fins if hungry.

LABYRINTH CATFISH (Clariidae)

"WALKING" CATFISH were imported from Southeast Asia several years ago. Those that escaped or were set free by their owners now pose a threat to the environments they have invaded.

These unusual fish have both gills and primitive lunglike organs. Swishing their tail and using their stout pectoral fins as "legs" to propel themselves, they can literally "walk" on land. In this way they escape when the waters they inhabit become unsuitable. During droughts, they stay moist by digging into mud and breathing atmospheric air. In or out of the water, their eight barbels aid in locating prey, whether eggs, insects, or fish twice their own size. They soon dominate whatever water they inhabit.

In community tanks, these catfish will attack and eat other fish, hence they must be kept isolated. They have ravenous appetites. The temperature of the water can be 50 to 95 degrees F. Cover the aquarium, but leave sufficient air space above to permit the fish to surface for breathing.

In many states, it is now illegal to possess these fish, so note their appearance. Their color variations include grays and browns.

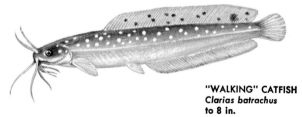

"WALKING" CATFISH
Clarias batrachus
to 8 in.

UPSIDE-DOWN CATFISH (Mochokidae)

AFRICAN POLKA-DOT CATFISH are rare and expensive, but they are desirable for a large community tank. They are hardy and peaceful, but they should be provided with hiding places. The water temperature should range from 72 to 80 degrees F. This species occasionally swims inverted or upside down.

UPSIDE-DOWN CATFISH have a dark belly and a light-colored back, opposite the usual coloring of a fish. This is an adaptation to their habit of swimming upside down. As the fish mature, they swim inverted more frequently. In a dimly lit, well-planted aquarium, a school of these fish will graze on algae and scavenge over surfaces. Note the large eyes of this species and also of the one above.

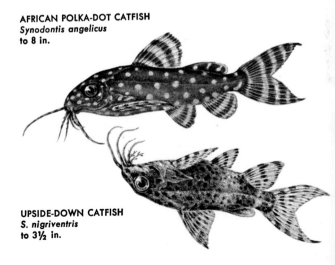

AFRICAN POLKA-DOT CATFISH
Synodontis angelicus
to 8 in.

UPSIDE-DOWN CATFISH
S. nigriventris
to 3½ in.

ELECTRIC CATFISH (Malapteruridae)

ELECTRIC CATFISH, the only species in its family, has electric organs similar to but weaker than those of electric eels (p. 67). The shock is strong enough to electrocute tiny fish, to numb large ones, and to startle an unwary handler. These fish are vicious and will attack all other fish. They must be isolated. The water should be neutral and 72 to 80 degrees F. Provide leafy plants for greens; also meaty and live foods.

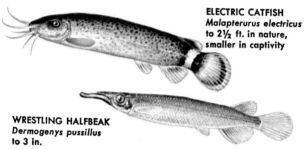

ELECTRIC CATFISH
Malapterurus electricus
to 2½ ft. in nature,
smaller in captivity

WRESTLING HALFBEAK
Dermogenys pussillus
to 3 in.

HALFBEAKS (Hemiramphidae)

WRESTLING HALFBEAKS, live-bearers imported from Southeast Asia, are not bred commercially. In Thailand, males are bred selectively for "fighting" contests in which a fighter locks his jaws around an opponent—a member of the same species. In home aquariums, keep the water at 68 to 72 degrees F.; add three fourths of a tablespoon of sea salt per gallon of water. These surface feeders must be given live foods. The "beak" is easily injured, so be careful in handling. These fish are short-lived.

STICKLEBACKS (Gasterosteidae)

FOUR-SPINED STICKLEBACKS are brackish-water fish that live in estuaries of the Atlantic along the northern coast of North America. The water should be conditioned with 1 tablespoon of sea salt per gallon of water. Its temperature should be 65 to 68 degrees F. At the breeding season, the colorful male builds a tunnel-nest of vegetation held together with sticky secretions. He and his mate enter the tunnel repeatedly. Each visit she lays eggs, and he fertilizes them. The male protects the eggs and then the young. This species is quarrelsome, so keep it isolated.

SEAHORSES AND PIPEFISHES (Syngnathidae)

PIPEFISH are in the same family as seahorses and often are considered marine fish. Like seahorses, they are covered with bony plates. Males cradle the eggs and the young in folds on their belly.

Sea salt must be added to the water in the tank. Follow the directions on the bag to get a salinity of about 1.018. Pipefish eat only live food, such as brine shrimp, *Daphnia,* and young live-bearers. The fish suck the food into their slim snout. Pipefish often swim vertically and may also jump out of the water.

FOUR-SPINED STICKLEBACK
Apeltes quadracus
to 2 in.

PIPEFISH
Syngnathus spicifer
to 6 in.

111

KILLIFISH OR TOOTHED CARPS (Cyprinodontidae)

Killifish lay eggs, though they belong to the same order as live-bearing fish (p. 118). More than 200 species, many of them colorful, occur in tropical and warm waters on all continents except Australia.

Killifish have a long body (from 1½ to 6 inches) and a flat head. They do not have barbels or an adipose fin. Killifish are not recommended for community tanks or for beginning aquarists.

SPANISH KILLIFISH, native to Spain and Algeria, live in the upper water levels. They inhabit brackish to marine waters. Keep two adult females (olive-green) for each mature male (blue-green). They may spawn in the plants. Feed them mostly live foods. If the fish appear to be sluggish, gradually add 1-2 teaspoons of sea salt for each gallon of water in the tank.

SPANISH KILLIFISH
Aphanius iberus
to 2 in.

RED LYRETAIL
Aphyosemion bivittatun
to 2½ in.

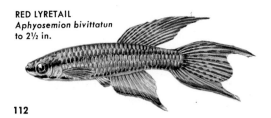

RED LYRETAILS are one of more than 20 species of *Aphyosemion* that are imported from Africa's west coast, east of Dahomey Gap. Most of the species are difficult to differentiate. They may interbreed, and their offspring are generally sterile.

The Red Lyretail needs a dimly lit tank with well-planted hiding areas. Keep this species in small groups consisting mainly of females. Hatchlings grow more slowly than do those of other members of the same genus. There are numerous and variously colored subspecies.

Killifish are more difficult to feed than are many fish. Many will accept only live foods, which are wholesome but impractical to provide. Those that become fussy about their eating may be persuaded to accept other foods by making only the alternate foods available. See basic diet (p. 28).

LYRETAILS do best in slightly acid, aged water that is treated with a teaspoon of sea salt per gallon. The water temperature should not exceed 75 degrees F. because warmth shortens their lifespan. Lights should be filtered through dense clumps of plants. For the bottom, where the fish will live, use fine sand or charcoal. Keep two or three females for each male. Males may fight. Eggs adhere to plants. Lyretails need plenty of live foods. In addition to the one shown, a golden variety is available.

LYRETAIL
A. australe
to 2½ in.

STEEL-BLUE APHYOSEMION is a lively, quarrelsome bottom dweller that is best kept isolated—one adult per tank. The aquarium should be shaded, the water aged and acid. A yellow variety is also available.

To prepare breeding tank, simmer peat (no additives) in boiled water. Press and cover with soft water. After the peat settles, introduce mature adults. The male chases his mate vigorously in courtship. Provide leafy plants in which she can rest, or supply male with two or three females.

Remove fertile eggs (not white) with a glass tube and place them in jars half filled with soft water to which a drop of 5 percent methylene blue is added. Store them in a dark, cool (70 degrees F.) place for three to seven weeks. To stimulate hatching, add a pinch of dried flake food on which bacteria feed and also begin to decompose the eggshells. Remove hatchlings from contaminated water at once.

BLUE GULARIS are quarrelsome, hardy eaters. Males are jewel-like. Color varieties are common. Give them the same care as above. Cover the tank!

STEEL-BLUE APHYOSEMION
Aphyosemion gardneri
to 2½ in.

BLUE GULARIS
A. sjoestedti
to 5½ in.

LINED PANCHAX
Aplocheilus lineatus
to 4 in.

ARGENTINE PEARL FISH
Cynolebias bellotti
to 3 in.

► **FIREMOUTH PANCHAX**
Epiplatys dageti
(formerly *E. chaperi*)
to 2½ in.

LINED PANCHAX , from Ceylon and India, lives mainly on insect larvae in nature, hence require live foods in aquariums. It is aggressive. Keep only with larger fish. Cover the tank! This species lives in upper water strata and spawns in floating plants.

ARGENTINE PEARL FISH live in ponds that dry up in summer. The adults die, but their eggs, buried in the mud, hatch when rains come again. To condition breeders, feed them live foods. Prepare peat (p. 114), and after the fish have spawned, remove them and siphon off the water. Seal the damp (not wet) peat in a plastic bag and store it in darkness for three to five months. Then submerge the peat in water, and the eggs will hatch. The voracious hatchlings mature in about eight weeks; they live only about eight months. Males fight.

FIREMOUTH PANCHAX should be fed mainly live foods. Two to three females and one male will school peacefully in a community tank.

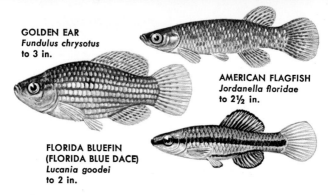

GOLDEN EAR
Fundulus chrysotus
to 3 in.

AMERICAN FLAGFISH
Jordanella floridae
to 2½ in.

FLORIDA BLUEFIN
(FLORIDA BLUE DACE)
Lucania goodei
to 2 in.

GOLDEN EARS, native to southeastern United States, are aggressive, so should not be kept with shy species. Mid-strata dwellers, they spawn in plants.

AMERICAN FLAGFISH are stout, hardy Florida fish. Males kept in the same quarters become antagonistic. After spawning, males protect and care for the brood. The young eat algae; adults are omnivorous.

FLORIDA BLUEFINS do best in roomy, well-planted tanks, the water not warmer than 70 degrees F. They live and spawn in plants in the top and middle strata. Females may lay several eggs daily for more than a month and will eat them if they are not removed. Protected eggs hatch in about two weeks.

MEDAKAS are peaceful, hardy fish—ideal for community tanks. In Japan, they live in paddies and are valued for eating mosquito larvae. Clusters of eggs stick to the female's vent and are fertilized there. They are then rubbed off onto plants. Shipments of deformed (humpbacked) specimens, unhealthy and usually sterile, are found occasionally in pet shops.

MEDAKA OR RICE FISH
Oryzias latipes
to 1½ in.

GOLDEN PHEASANT
Roloffia occidentalis
to 3½ in.

GOLDEN PHEASANT is rowdy, hence not a community fish. The water should be about 72 degrees F. Breeding is the same as for Argentine Pearl Fish (p. 115), but damp periods last a month or two longer. It lives in lower water strata. Feed it live foods.

FOUR-EYED FISH (Anablepidae)

FOUR-EYED FISH are difficult to keep in an aquarium. They feed in schools as they skim just beneath the surface. With their bulging eyes, they can see either in air or in water. A show-type tank of at least 50 gallons is needed. The water should be 72 to 75 degrees F. Feed them a varied diet. The sexual organs of these fish are tilted to the left or to the right. A "left" female can copulate only with a "right" male and vice versa. They are live-bearers.

FOUR-EYED FISH
Anableps anableps
to 12 in.

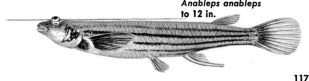

117

LIVEBEARERS (Poecillidae)

Livebearers are native to North and South America and the West Indies. They are shoalers that inhabit shallow waters, usually close either to deep water or to dense plants in which they can take refuge. Hardy and easy for beginners to manage, livebearers are the most popular of all aquarium fish except Goldfish. They rarely exceed three inches in length, making them ideal for most home aquariums. Their lifespan is only two or three years, but these fish are so prolific that they produce many generations in their lifetime, thus perpetuating themselves.

Livebearers bear their young alive, the fertilized eggs developing in the female's ovary. Information on caring for livebearers is on p. 120.

PIKE TOP MINNOW, from South and Central America, is exceptionally large for a poecillid. It requires a tank of 50 gallons, with the water at 75 to 85 degrees F. and two or three teaspoons of sea salt added per gallon. Other livebearers are omnivorous, but the Pike Top Minnow is carnivorous. Its rapacity and large-toothed mouth make it a threat to defenseless neighbors, particularly young fish. Even fellow Pikes may be assaulted. The species is prolific, but it will gobble up its own unprotected young. Pikes are an inch long at birth. Undernourished mothers produce stillborns.

PIKE TOP MINNOW
Belonesox belizanus
to 8 in.

All livebearing males develop a "gonopodium." With this organ, an extension of the anal fin, the male deposits sperm in females' oviducts.

**GAMBUSIA
(MOSQUITOFISH)**
Gambusia affinus
male, to 1¼ in.
female, to 2½ in.

DWARF TOPMINNOW
Heterandria formosa
male, to ¾ in.
female, to 1½ in.

GAMBUSIAS, natives of southern United States, have been introduced throughout the world to aid in control of mosquitoes, especially where malaria and yellow fever are a threat. These tiny fish can eat daily their own weight in mosquito larvae or pupae. Though drab, Gambusias are interesting and easy to keep in an aquarium. There should be at least three females for each male. Females are similar to the female guppy but have dark specks on their tail. Isolation is necessary because these fish bite the fins of other fish. Parents eat their young. Gambusias were the first of the livebearers offered for sale to hobbyists. A marbled variety has been developed.

DWARF TOPMINNOWS, natives of southeastern United States, are the smallest of all livebearing animals and are also one of the smallest of all living vertebrates. These active fish are suitable for even the smallest aquarium. The ideal water temperature is 70 degrees F. but can range from 55 to 95. Because the embryos develop in separate stages, only a few babies are born each day for one or two weeks. A month after the last baby is born, births may begin again. If well fed, the parents will not consume their offspring.

GUPPIES are the favorites of all the tropical fish. They are peaceful, friendly, hardy, and so prolific that one pair can fill an aquarium with offspring in a short time. They are valued for mosquito control and for live food for other fish. In aquariums, always have a majority of females. Need basic diet.

Male guppies are forever courting. If a female remains stationary and her partner contacts her vent with his gonopodium, she is fertilized. The sperm is preserved in the female's oviduct, and so even after males are removed, a female is capable of having six or more broods. Gestation averages a month but can be much longer, depending on the time of year, health of the female, and conditions in the tank.

A pregnant female can be identified by the gravid spot (darkened area) behind her anal fin just posterior to the belly. When viewed from above, her sides appear swollen. To prepare her for delivery, keep the female in shallow (about 8 in.), aged water at 75 to 80 degrees F. Provide floating plants at least two inches thick into which the newborn can scurry, for even the mother will eat them. If other fish must be kept in the same tank, feed them heavily to suppress their hunger. Disturbing a pregnant female may result in premature deliveries. One female may have as many as 200 babies; the average is 40 to 50. Young females have smaller litters. All of the newborn are about a quarter of an inch long. Feed them small meals at least three times daily.

Guppies live about two years. Breeders have developed multitudes of fin colors and patterns. Many clubs breed what they believe are excellent specimens and then hold guppy shows to display them.

GUPPY
Poecilia reticulata
(formerly *Lebistes*)
male, to 1½ in.
female, to 2½ in.

Red Deltatail

Cobra Robsontail

Blue Veiltail

Halfblack Veiltail

**Gold Flamingo
Roundtail**

Varicolored Flagtail

TAIL SHAPES

round

pin

flag

robson

top sword

triangle

spade

bottom sword

veil

spear

double

fan

lyre

delta

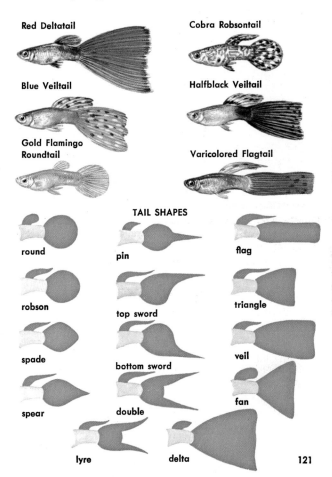

BLACK-BELLIED LIMIA
Limia melanogaster
(also *Poecilia melanogaster*)
to 2 in.

BLACK-BELLIED LIMIA'S name refers to the permanent black gravid spot on the female. These peaceful fish are from Jamaica. Care for them as for other live-bearers. They seldom have more than 40 babies at once, and the young grow slowly.

MOLLIES, from Central and South America, are often sold inexpensively as fish for beginners. This is unfortunate, for unless given special care, the fish will perish. To ready an aquarium for Mollies, fill it with slightly alkaline, aged water, adding two to three teaspoons of sea salt per gallon. Keep the temperature between 73 and 75 degrees F. As with all live-bearers, provide the basic diet, but in addition, make certain that vegetable matter is available daily. Without algae, the fish will be unhealthy. If disturbed, pregnant females will miscarry or die.

The plastic bags in which shipments of Mollies arrive in stores are often populated with newborn fry. If the adults are well fed, they will not eat their young. Mollies are sensitive to common fish diseases (p. 34), so treat newly acquired fish with methylene blue tonic.

All of the many available varieties of mollies will interbreed, but their offspring may be sterile. Commercially raised varieties usually lack the high dorsal fins of wild specimens. Many live for about three years.

GREEN SAILFIN MOLLY
Poecilia latipinna
(formerly *Mollienisia*)
to 4 in.

BLACK MOLLY
P. sphenops
to 2½ in.

**OTHER VARIETIES
OF THE
BLACK MOLLY**

Black Lyretail
to 3½ in.

Marble
to 2½ in.

Sphenop or Orange-tail
to 2½ in.

SWORDTAIL
Xiphophorus helleri
to 5 in.

SWORDTAILS were imported originally from Mexico. They were the green variety. Since then, their flashy appearance and many variations have made them one of the most popular of all aquarium fish. Provide one to two gallons of water per fish. The water should be slightly hard (pH of 7.2), and its temperature should be maintained between 72 and 78 degrees F. Cover the tank, for these fish are accomplished jumpers. Feed them the basic diet at least twice daily. Usually only males have the extended tail fin or "sword." Individuals vary in temperament, but males frequently fight. Keep one male with more than two females in each tank.

Breeding is the same as for guppies (p. 120). Broods of more than a hundred are not uncommon, but parents may quickly reduce this number by eating their young. A lack of hormones may cause some adult females to revert to males.

New varieties appear on the market regularly. Hybrids are developed by crossing with other Swordtails and also with Platys (p. 126). Shades of red, as one example, may vary from a true red to a velvet red or a brick red.

VARIETIES OF SWORDTAILS

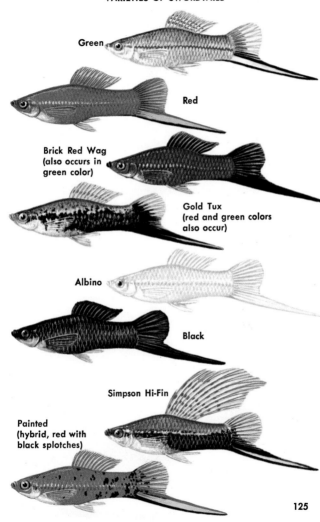

Green

Red

Brick Red Wag
(also occurs in
green color)

Gold Tux
(red and green colors
also occur)

Albino

Black

Simpson Hi-Fin

Painted
(hybrid, red with
black splotches)

PLATY
Xiphophorus maculatus
to 3 in.

PLATYS, from Mexico and Guatamala, are peaceful community fish. Care and breeding is the same as for other livebearers. Selective breeding has produced many varieties. Those illustrated are only a few of the most common. The shades of the colors may vary as well as the markings.

VARIATUS, from the same region as the Platy, has a longer dorsal fin and a more elongated body. Care and breeding are the same as for other livebearers.

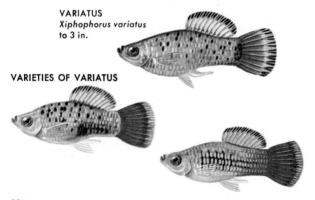

VARIATUS
Xiphophorus variatus
to 3 in.

VARIETIES OF VARIATUS

VARIETIES OF PLATYS
(others are possible)

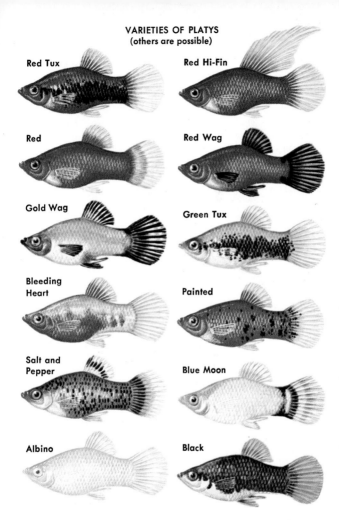

Red Tux

Red Hi-Fin

Red

Red Wag

Gold Wag

Green Tux

Bleeding Heart

Painted

Salt and Pepper

Blue Moon

Albino

Black

GLASSFISH (Centropomidae)

INDIAN GLASSFISH are numerous in fresh waters of India and nearby regions. In aquariums, use medium-hard water, well aged with two to three teaspoons of salt per gallon of water. Initially these fish are timid, but they become quite tame. Hatchlings are so tiny they are difficult to feed. Only males have the blue edging on the rays of their fins. The gray organ visible inside the fish is the swim bladder.

TIGER FISH (Theraponidae)

TIGER FISH are a recent importation. Young specimens (about 3 inches) are expensive. Given adequate space (a 50 gallon tank) and plenty of food, they grow quickly. Keep them with fish of equal size. Tigers that are not comfortable and well fed lose their color, becoming faded-out black fish. A 15-inch Tiger Fish may eat several three-inch Goldfish daily and be always hungry for more.

SUNFISH (Centrarchidae)

SUNFISH are collected in quiet waters of North America. Once secure, with hiding places nearby, they lose their shyness. Note the large gill covers. These fish have the unusual habit of waddling along the bottom on their pectoral fins. Keep them with sunfish of the same size. In established tanks, new members are not tolerated. Eggs hatch in less than a week. Males protect both the eggs and the young. Water kept at room temperature is suitable. It should be near neutral in pH.

INDIAN GLASSFISH
Chanda ranga
to 2 in.

SIAMESE TIGER FISH
Datnioides microlepis
to 16 in.

EVERGLADES PYGMY SUNFISH
Elassoma evergladei
to 1¼ in.

BLACKBANDED SUNFISH
Mesogonistius chaetodon
to 3 in.

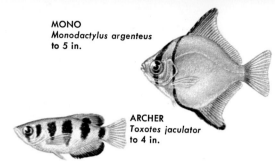

MONO
Monodactylus argenteus
to 5 in.

ARCHER
Toxotes jaculator
to 4 in.

FINGERFISH (Monodactylidae)

MONOS, from the brackish coastal waters of eastern Africa to Malaysia, require a spacious tank containing aged water to which three teaspoons of salt per gallon have been added. These fish do best in schools. Quick movements outside the tank may cause them to panic and injure themselves. They can be kept with other brackish-water fish. Feed them an abundance of live foods, and keep the temperature of the water at 75 degrees F.

ARCHERFISH (Toxotidae)

ARCHERS, natives of brackish waters in the Indo-Australian region, cannot be provided with conditions in a normal tank to permit watching them "spit" down insects from above the water. They are accurate to a distance of about five feet and even allow for the reflection of light in water as they make their aim. Keep them in aged water to which two teaspoons of salt per gallon have been added. The temperature of the water should be 78 to 80 degrees F.

ARGUS FISH (Scatophagidae)

SCATS come from tropical Indo-Pacific estuaries. Keep them in water that has a temperature of about 75 degrees F. Buy at least two young. Ask at what salinity they have been living and duplicate it. For every inch of growth thereafter add a half to a full teaspooon of sea salt until a measurement of 1.018 density is reached. (A hydrometer, available at pet shops, gives this measurement.)

Scats are peaceful and become quite tame. Feed them the basic diet, adding daily doses of vegetable matter. Unsatisfactory conditions often result in Ich disease (p. 35). Markings on this fish are variable. The fin spines are venomous.

LEAF FISH (Nandidae)

LEAF FISH, from South America, looks remarkably like a dead leaf floating slowly in the water. Though the fish appears delicate and harmless, it is actually predatory and must be fed enormous amounts of live foods. A Leaf Fish can eat its own weight in Guppies daily. Keep the temperature of the water at 72 to 76 degrees F. Young have white specks.

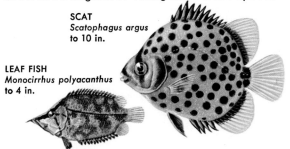

SCAT
Scatophagus argus
to 10 in.

LEAF FISH
Monocirrhus polyacanthus
to 4 in.

CICHLIDS (Cichlidae)

Cichlids usually from either South or Central America, have well-developed lips and only one nostril on each side of the head. The head, eyes, and scales are large, and the lateral line is divided in the middle. The anterior rays of the dorsal and anal fins are spiny. Older fish develop a spinal hump and rough scales; they do not close their mouth in respiration.

For most cichlids, a tank smaller than 15 gallons is cramping. Gravel should be medium to coarse. For decoration, use well-anchored, heavy objects. Large cichlids will break heaters.

Cichlids are believed by many to be the most intelligent of all fish. Their behavior varies with the species and the individual. A breeding pair tests their compatibility by locking jaws and tugging at each other. If one partner breaks this test, it may be attacked by the other. If the "kiss" is favorable, the pair establishes a spawning territory. For several days they scrape a spawning site to clean it.

In both sexes, small tubes develop at the vent. The female deposits a layer of eggs on the cleaned surface, and the male promptly fertilizes them. Both parents fan the eggs, removing any that are infertile or infested with fungus. At 80 degrees F., hatching occurs in five days. The parents pick up the hatchlings in their mouths and move them to pits in the gravel. In the process, they scour the young by a chewing action. The free-swimming babies later school around their parents. If a baby wanders away, a parent sucks it up at once and squirts it back into the school. Cichlids do not mate for life, but in aquariums, compatible pairs mate repeatedly

BLUE ACARA
Aequidens pulcher
(formerly *A. latifrons*)
to 6 in.

KEYHOLE CICHLID
A. maronii
to 4 in.

PORT
A. portalegrensis
to 6 in.

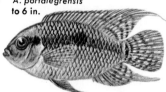

BLUE ACARAS, from South America, enjoy grubbing in the gravel. This kicks up large amounts of dirt, so keep the water filtered with an auxiliary outside or corner filter. Add about a third fresh water bimonthly. Except when they are excited, the older fish do not have the dark vertical bars that are prominent in the young.

KEYHOLE CICHLIDS live in streams in northern South America. They can be kept in community tanks, for they seldom dig in gravel or uproot plants. These are shy fish that need hiding places. The "keyhole" blotch may or may not be conspicuous. Clean water is required; ideal temperature 80 degrees F.

PORTS are named for the locality where they were first found—Porto Alegre, Brazil. Their original popularity climbed because of their ease in breeding and their devotion in parenthood. Ports dig, especially at breeding time. Temperature of the water should be 70 to 80 degrees F.

AGASSIZ'S DWARF CICHLIDS are shy fish of streams of tropical South America. In aquariums, they rarely uproot plants, which provide ideal hiding places for them. The water should be soft—slightly acid. Females lay red eggs in caves or in dense growths of plants. After he fertilizes the eggs, the male is banished by his partner. Remove him from the tank. Females may eat their first spawn but care for subsequent broods. Species easily contracts Ich disease (p. 35). Add medications gradually.

YELLOW DWARF CICHLIDS, also from South America, are a relatively peaceful fish, hence can be kept in a community tank. They prefer soft, slightly acid water at 80 degrees F. Of all the dwarf cichlids, they are the best parents. The male is often allowed to share in the domestic chores—the rearing of the young.

AGASSIZ'S DWARF CICHLID
Apistogramma agassizi
male, to 3 in.
female, to 2 in.

YELLOW DWARF CICHLID
A. pertense
male, to 2 in.
female, to 1¼ in.

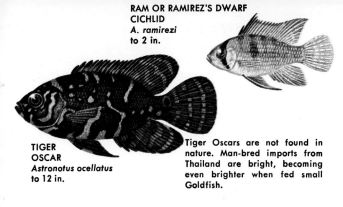

RAM OR RAMIREZ'S DWARF CICHLID
A. ramirezi
to 2 in.

TIGER OSCAR
Astronotus ocellatus
to 12 in.

Tiger Oscars are not found in nature. Man-bred imports from Thailand are bright, becoming even brighter when fed small Goldfish.

RAMS, still another South American cichlid, are un-tunately often as anxious to eat their eggs as they are to lay them. Remove spawn-eating parents, and rear the eggs artificially by allowing air bubbles to circulate water (not bubbles!) over them. Remove white eggs. Hatching occurs in three days. Rams usually live only two years. They are sensitive to Ich disease (p. 35).

OSCAR, from the large rivers of the South American tropics, has climbed in popularity in recent years. The breeding of new color and pattern varieties has put them more in demand. Owners commonly boast of the intelligence and individuality of these pets. Oscars are heavy eaters and grow fast on a diet of large morsels of prepared food and smaller live food. They breed in the usual cichlid manner and are model parents. Water conditions are not too critical, but a baby an inch long will require at least 50 gallons in a year, when he is grown. Heaters are not necessary for adults.

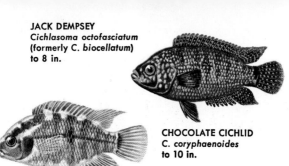

JACK DEMPSEY
Cichlasoma octofasciatum
(formerly *C. biocellatum*)
to 8 in.

CHOCOLATE CICHLID
C. coryphaenoides
to 10 in.

JACK DEMPSEYS, from Central America, were named after the heavyweight boxing champion. Their aggressiveness diminishes in tanks exceeding 25 gallons, but these fish are definitely not for community tanks. With watchfulness, they can be kept with Dempseys of equal size. Jack Dempseys are fond of digging and destroying plants. Their gravel can be leveled in the morning, but by evening it is again mountainous. Colors intensify at breeding or feeding times. Pets become quite tame and may live as long as ten years.

CHOCOLATE CICHLIDS, from the Amazon region of South America, are among the most quarrelsome of all the cichlids. Amateurs are shocked when their shy inch-long baby grows (if space allows) into a ten-inch monster that does not even get along with its own kind. One partner may be killed during courtship. Feed large morsels of food, such as earthworms, chunks of beef heart, and small live fish. The water temperature should be 78 to 80 degrees F. These fish quickly deepen or fade in color.

RED DEVILS are not for the average fish hobbyist. Grown adults need 100-gallon tanks and a constant supply of live foods. They are occasionally seen in public aquariums. Natural light enhances their contrasting black and red, which in some varieties may tend to be a faded orange. Some varieties also lack the large lips characteristic of the species. Their range is Central America.

FESTIVUMS are prevalent in their native habitat in the Amazon River. They are often found schooling with Angelfish (p. 142), and the two can also be mixed in captivity. Plant their aquarium heavily and keep it well aerated with clean water at 80 degrees F. The shy, flighty adults make unsatisfactory parents. Eggs should be reared artificially (p. 135). Hatchlings are delicate.

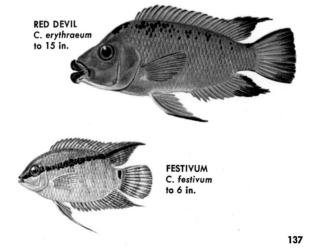

RED DEVIL
C. erythraeum
to 15 in.

FESTIVUM
C. festivum
to 6 in.

FIREMOUTH individuals vary in temperament from pugnacious to peaceful. It is difficult to pair compatible breeders, but once established, they are good parents. If they become excited, they may distend a bright red membranous area of skin below the throat. Firemouths are from Central America and Mexico.

CONVICTS, from Central America, are typical scrappy cichlids. Their digging and mauling of plants quickly upsets a nicely arranged aquarium. Smaller fish are attacked. In nature, Convicts are striped. Commercial breeders propagate albinos.

SEVERUMS, natives of northern South America, are peaceful when young, resembling Discus (p. 144). On a hardy diet, young Severums grow quickly into powerful adults. Native adults are gray with red spots. An albino variety is now commonly sold in pet shops.

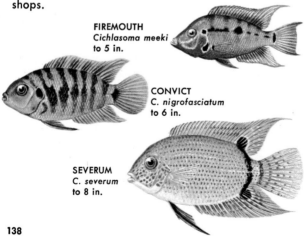

FIREMOUTH
Cichlasoma meeki
to 5 in.

CONVICT
C. nigrofasciatum
to 6 in.

SEVERUM
C. severum
to 8 in.

CHECKERBOARD CICHLID
Crenicara maculata
to 4 in.

PIKE CICHLID
Crenicichla lepidota
to 8 in.

ORANGE CHROMADE
Etroplus maculatus
to 3 in.

CHECKERBOARD CICHLIDS are not commonly found in stores. Pairs spawn in caves, and broods are successfully reared now and then. These fish are drab in badly managed tanks that are sparsely planted.

PIKE CICHLID is one of the many elongated cichlids from tropical South America. It engulfs unsuspecting prey swiftly. The tail of an oversized victim eventually disappears as the meal is downed in gulps. Pikes spawn in pits, and males assume rearing responsibilities. Cover the tank.

ORANGE CHROMADES are natives of India. Commercial breeders use one teaspoon of salt per gallon of water, which is maintained at 80 degrees F. Eggs are laid on concealed surfaces in the usual cichlid manner, and the non-swimming fry are attached on short threads. The young feed on parental slime (p. 144).

DIRTEATER
Geophagus jurupari
to 10 in.

EGYPTIAN MOUTHBROODER
Hemihaplochromis multicolor
(formerly *Haplochromis
multicolor*)
to 3 in.

DIRTEATERS, natives of the tropics of northern South America, habitually plunge their pointed snout into the bottom and scoop up a mouthful of gravel. They sift out food particles in the gravel, which is then spewed from the gill covers. Because of this, provision the aquarium with smooth, round pebbles. Substrate filters are undesirable. These peaceful mouthbrooders occasionally breed in captivity.

EGYPTIAN MOUTHBROODERS do not breed in the usual cichlid manner. A prospective male digs a pit and then forcefully coaxes his mate into it. After her eggs are laid, the female gobbles them up and stores them in her throat sac. Decoyed by "egg spots" on the male's anal fin, the female comes close to the male to suck up any overlooked "eggs." He then releases sperm and fertilizes the eggs. After this occurs, remove the male. For two weeks the female incubates the eggs in her mouth, and during this time, she does not eat. By a chewing action, she cleans and aerates the eggs. For about a week after hatching, the free-swimming fry use the female's mouth as a place of refuge.

AFRICAN JEWELFISH are pugnacious cichlids that attack other fish. They also dig in the bottom. Typical of the group, however, they are model parents. They breed easily in aquariums and in the usual cichlid manner. At breeding time, they change from a drab green to a strawberry red. Over-anxious males may attack and kill unwilling females. By the time the babies from a brood are two months old, they are assaulting each other. Water composition is not critical, but its temperature should be about 78 degrees F.

AFRICAN PURPLE CICHLIDS require an established aquarium with water that is soft and slightly acid at 80 degrees F. A teaspoon of sea salt per gallon is recommended for their well-being. Spawning is cichlid-like, with the eggs being placed on shady surfaces—such as the inside of a plant pot. The famale protects her young and may become so upset by her mate's presence that he must be removed before she hurts him. The young are very delicate.

AFRICAN JEWELFISH
Hemichromis bimaculatus
to 5 in.

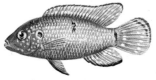

AFRICAN PURPLE CICHLID
Pelmatochromis pulcher
to 4 in.

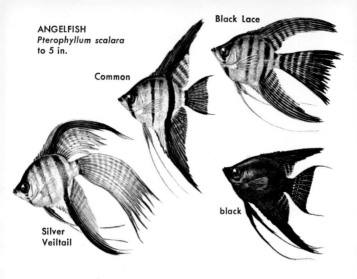

ANGELFISH
Pterophyllum scalara
to 5 in.

Black Lace

Common

Silver
Veiltail

black

ANGELFISH are known to anyone who has owned an aquarium. These cichlids are peace-loving and non-destructive. Occasionally a large Angelfish becomes aggressive. They thrive in the normal conditions of a well-managed tropical fish community tank in which there are other quiet fish. The water should be 75 to 85 degrees F. and barely acid.

Thousands of Angelfish are bred annually by commercial fish dealers. In a home aquarium, it is a rewarding experience to watch two well-paired Angels spawn on an Amazon Plant or on a strip of slate that is slightly angled against the glass. The rearing of the family by the parents can also be observed. Some are poor parents, however.

Eggs can be reared artificially by placing the leaf or the egg-covered slate in fresh tap water that has

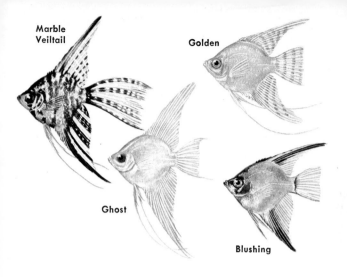

Marble Veiltail

Golden

Ghost

Blushing

been allowed to reach the same temperature as the spawning tank. Air bubbles should circulate water past the eggs but not touch them. Hatching will occur in two or three days. As soon as their yolk sac is dissolved, the newly hatched, free-swimming fry should be fed brine shrimp and other fine foods.

It is not unusual for two female cichlids to breed simply to rid themselves of eggs. If infertile eggs are produced repeatedly, try replacing a partner. One of the pair may be sterile.

Angels tire of repetitious diets and may quit eating. Feed them a varied menu from the basic diet. Newly acquired specimens are shy, but they soon become tame enough to accept food from the fingers. Many varieties of Angelfish have been developed from the original Silver strain.

DISCUS, from the Amazon region, are for the advanced aquarium hobbyist. The water must be soft, acid in pH, and 80 degrees F. Hard, alkaline water will kill these fish. Freshen a third of the water with new, aged water three times a month. One teaspoon of sea salt per gallon helps prevent sickness. If new specimens are infected with "worms" (protozoans) around head, treat with antibiotics (p. 33). Plants provide security. Adults need a tank of 50 gallons or more. Feed a varied diet with plenty of live foods in frequent small meals.

Discus are peaceful fish, but pairs should be isolated at breeding. They spawn like other cichlids and care for their broods. Artificial rearing is unwise, for as soon as the young are free-swimming, they feed on a slime secreted from the parents' skin, browsing off first one parent and then the other. After about a week, begin feeding newly hatched brine shrimp, rinsed in fresh water.

BROWN SCHULTZ
*Symphysodon
aequifasciata*
to 8 in.

BLUE SCHULTZ
(variety of *S. aequifasciata*)

RAINBOW SCHULTZ
(variety of *S. aequifasciata*)

RED HECKLE DISCUS
S. discus
to 8 in.

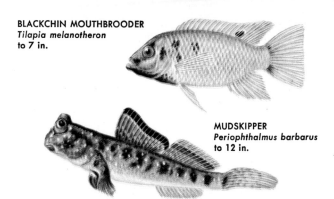

BLACKCHIN MOUTHBROODER
Tilapia melanotheron
to 7 in.

MUDSKIPPER
Periophthalmus barbarus
to 12 in.

BLACKCHIN MOUTHBROODERS are abundant in lakes and rivers of Africa. This species is often transplanted for rearing in ponds as a food fish. In aquariums, augment their diet with ample amounts of plant matter. Eggs are fertilized where they are laid, then incubated and cared for as in the Egyptian Mouthbrooder (p. 140)—except the male incubates the eggs.

MUDSKIPPERS (Periophthalmidae)

MUDSKIPPERS have bulging eyes that emerge first when these fish come out of the water of the mangrove swamps where they live. They walk or jump on their pectoral fins—"skipping" across the mudflats. They pause in muddy pools to wet their gills. They may even climb onto logs or rocks to bask but jump back into pools when alarmed. Tanks should be covered and partly terrestrial, with pools of water four to six inches deep. Add two teaspoons of sea salt per gallon of water.

CLIMBING PERCH
Anabas testudineus
to 8 in.

LABYRINTHFISHES (Anabantidae)

Fish in this family gulp atmospheric air into a labyrinth of storage chambers above the gills. The oxygen in this stored air supplements that absorbed by the gills in respiration. Older fish rely wholly on this air and will drown if they do not have surface air to breathe. If the air is much colder than the water, the fish develop respiratory illnesses. Cover the tank. Labyrinthfishes are available at any fish store. They are ideal for beginners. In a well-managed community tank, they commonly live for more than five years. They are peaceful, though two adult males of the same species will fight. They are omnivorous. Most species in this family build bubble nests for breeding.

CLIMBING PERCHES (not true perches) are a food fish in Asia. In captivity, these predators can leap through small gaps. Propelling themselves on their gill plates and pectoral fins, they will then "walk" away. Eggs float randomly until hatching.

BETTA, or Fighting Fish, males are unmannerly only toward other male Bettas. Condition these fish with a basic diet that is high in live food. The temperature of the water should be 80 degrees F. Do not put a male and a female together unless they are ready to breed. In shallow, still water, a male will prepare a foamy bubble nest. A distended, ready female will follow her flamboyant male to this nest.

146

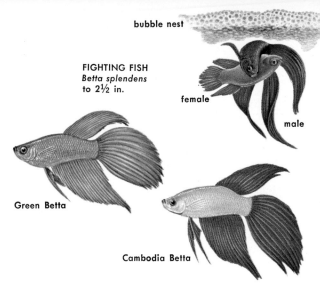

bubble nest

FIGHTING FISH
Betta splendens
to 2½ in.

female

male

Green Betta

Cambodia Betta

Some Asian peoples stage public fighting contests between male Bettas. Over the years of selective breeding, many varieties of fins and colors have been achieved for this species. Do not mistake a short-finned immature male for a female. Males only a few weeks old will fight each other. Females never fight. Males keep their bubble nest in repair and fry in place until they leave the nest.

After a spawning embrace, which may last totally for hours, the female releases eggs, which the male immediately fertilizes. Before the eggs sink, the male catches them in his mouth and "blows" them into the nest. After spawning is completed, remove female. Place her in medicated water to heal any torn fins. Males care for spawn and also for young until they are free-swimming. Then remove male. Young fish's first food is infusoria. Feed often. Bettas are old at two years.

DWARF HONEY GOURAMIS, native to northeastern India, have gained popularity recently. They are peaceful but shy, needing hiding places to escape real or imagined dangers. Males often reinforce their bubble nest with bits of plant material. Both sexes normally have a dark stripe along their flanks. At spawning time, the female's stripe fades, and the male's deepens in color.

GIANT GOURAMIS are by no means the "giants" of the gourami world, for Kissing Gouramis grow to twice their length. Though prolific, many males are poor nest builders. Bubbles are scattered in floating plants. Eggs usually float up into the nest from the parents spawning below. Males spray a stream of fine bubbles over the nest periodically.

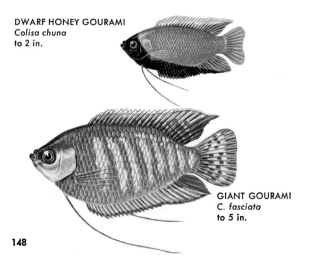

DWARF HONEY GOURAMI
Colisa chuna
to 2 in.

GIANT GOURAMI
C. fasciata
to 5 in.

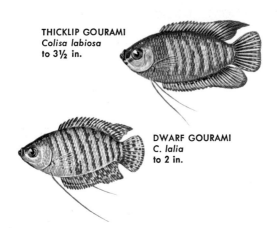

THICKLIP GOURAMI
Colisa labiosa
to 3½ in.

DWARF GOURAMI
C. lalia
to 2 in.

THICKLIP GOURAMIS occasionally show up with other gourami shipments but are not usually for sale in large numbers. The narrow dark band around their lips makes their lips appear heavier than they are. In a community tank of 15 gallons or larger and kept well fed on a basic diet, these are peaceful fish. Males anchor their bubble nest haphazardly in surface plants. During spawning, eggs float up into or are spit into the nest.

DWARF GOURAMIS are shy but peaceful and desirable. The male constructs his bubble nest painstakingly, weaving into it pieces of leaves, algae, and twigs for reinforcement. Nests of other species cover a larger surface area and fall apart after the eggs hatch, but the male Dwarf Gourami's nest has a small diameter, is deep, and remains intact long after the young depart. The basic diet must be augmented with vegetation.

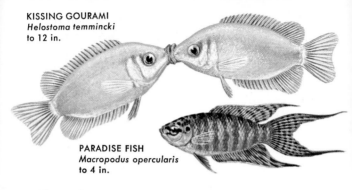

KISSING GOURAMI
Helostoma temmincki
to 12 in.

PARADISE FISH
Macropodus opercularis
to 4 in.

KISSING GOURAMIS are known for their habit of extending their thick fleshy lips and kissing. This kissing is not believed to be linked with sex, for even immature Kissing Gouramis seem to enjoy "kissing." Keep these fish in tanks of at least 20 gallons, and satisfy their huge appetites by serving meals at least twice daily. Vegetable matter should be added as a supplement at least one meal. Kissing Gouramis engage in the typical spawning embraces of labyrinthfishes, but they do not build a bubble nest. Large fish may produce a thousand eggs that float randomly until hatching.

PARADISE FISH have such undesirable temperaments that their popularity has greatly diminished. The temperature of the water must not exceed 75 degrees F. Meaty foods are an essential in their basic diet. Paradise Fish fight either by locking jaws in the usual cichlid fashion or by biting their opponent's flanks. Males attack other fish and guard their nest viciously. An albino variety of this species is also available.

PEARL GOURAMIS are pleasing pets. Though shy at first, they become quite tame and easy to keep in meduim-sized community tanks. They will seldom attack other fish. The male is a gentleman during courtship, not driving the female too hard and not nipping her fins. Remove the female and other fish after spawning is completed so that the male can guard his large bubble nest in peace. This species is also called Lace Gourami or Mosaic Gourami. Prime males have red chests.

MOONLIGHT GOURAMIS are a food fish in their native Thailand. Care and disposition are the same as for the previous species, but large specimens may pick on smaller more docile species. These fish are almost full grown before they reach sexual maturity and breed. Their shimmering, metallic silver color results from the reflection of light from their numerous tiny scales.

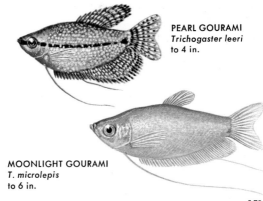

PEARL GOURAMI
Trichogaster leeri
to 4 in.

MOONLIGHT GOURAMI
T. microlepis
to 6 in.

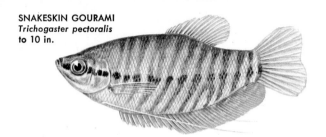

SNAKESKIN GOURAMI
Trichogaster pectoralis
to 10 in.

SNAKESKIN GOURAMIS, among the largest of the gouramis, are considered to be the most peaceful and gentle of the group. A family of these fish can be raised in a tank without worry of cannibalism. They are bubble nest builders. The modified pelvic fins, or feelers, are common to all gouramis. They can be moved in any direction to help the fish test and sense his environment.

BLUE GOURAMIS, the most popular of all the gouramis, are hardy, inexpensive, prolific, and easy to raise. They are sometimes kept in large schools of predominantly females. Encounters may occur between males, but usually no harm results. Adult males have a long, pointed dorsal fin; in females, the dorsal fin is rounded. Blue Gouramis breed by producing a large bubble nest and then spawning in the usual labyrinthfish fashion. The bubble nest gives the fry an adequate supply of oxygen.

Blue Gouramis are often put in aquariums to eat *Hydra*, which may be dangerous to all of the young fish. Gouramis also reduce an overpopulation of snails. They must be provided with the basic diet, however. Of the several color and pattern varieties, the most common is the Opaline Gourami.

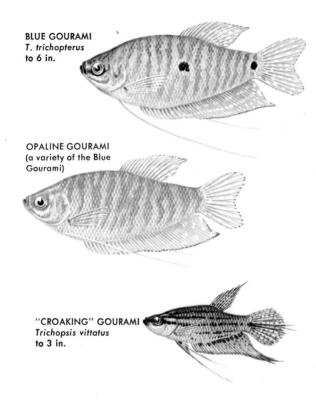

BLUE GOURAMI
T. trichopterus
to 6 in.

OPALINE GOURAMI
(a variety of the Blue
Gourami)

"CROAKING" GOURAMI
Trichopsis vittatus
to 3 in.

"CROAKING" GOURAMI is the name earned by the male of this species. During courtship or when confronted by another male, he makes a croaking or purring sound by gulping in air. The male often constructs his bubble nest under leaves. After spawning, female may be permitted to help gather sinking eggs for placing them in the nest.

SILVERSIDES (Antherinidae)

DWARF AUSTRALIAN RAINBOW FISH are peaceful, active schoolers of community tanks. One teaspoon of sea salt per gallon of water is beneficial. Eggs are laid in plants on several consecutive mornings, and if not eaten, they hatch in one or two weeks.

SOLES (Soleidae)

DWARF FLOUNDERS are inactive, bottom-dwelling flatfish. Young flounders are normal in shape, but as they grow, they turn onto their side, their eye also migrating so that it is on top. Their mouth also twists. Feed these fish the basic diet. Provide them with sand in which they can dig and camouflage themselves. Use one teaspoon of sea salt per gallon of water to provide proper salinity.

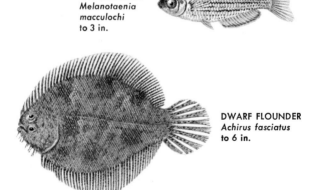

DWARF AUSTRALIAN
RAINBOWFISH
*Melanotaenia
macculochi*
to 3 in.

DWARF FLOUNDER
Achirus fasciatus
to 6 in.

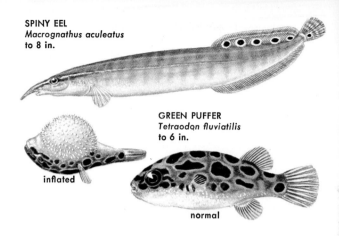

SPINY EEL
Macrognathus aculeatus
to 8 in.

GREEN PUFFER
Tetraodon fluviatilis
to 6 in.

inflated

normal

SPINY EELS (Mastocembelidae)

SPINY EELS have an elongated, rounded body, but they are not true eels. They are nocturnal. In bright light, they hide under the gravel with just their snout protruding. Feed mixed foods. Their favorites are worms and tiny fishes. Cover the tank completely, for these fish can slither out of any gaps.

PUFFERS (Tetraodontidae)

PUFFERS become nippy toward other fish as they grow older, hence they should be kept in isolated tanks. Their water should be salty—a teaspoon of sea salt for each gallon of water. A flower pot covered with algae and set on its side will provide a secure home as well as some vegetation on which to nibble. Feed them such live foods as snails, mealworms, tubifex worms, and earthworms.

FOR MORE INFORMATION

Aquarium Journal, San Francisco Aquarium Society, Steinhart Aquarium, San Francisco, Calif.

Aquarium Magazine, Lil & Len Rubin, Maywood, N.J.

Axelrod, Emmens, Scuttherpe, Vorderwinkler, Pronek, **Exotic Tropical Fishes**, TFH Publications, Inc., Englewood Cliffs, N.J., 1961.

Axelrod, Herbert R. and Leonard Schultz, **Handbook of Tropical Aquarium Fishes**, McGraw-Hill Book Co., Inc., N.Y., 1955.

The Complete Aquarist's Guide to Freshwater Tropical Fishes, edited by John Gilbert, Golden Press, N.Y., 1970.

Conroy, D.A. and R.L. Herman, **Textbook of Fish Diseases**, TFH Publications, Inc., Englewood Cliffs, N.J., 1970.

Dogiel, V.A., **Parasitology of Fishes**, TFH Publications, Inc., Englewood Cliffs, N.J., 1961.

Goldstein, Robert J., **Anabantoids Gouramis and Related Fishes**, TFH Publications, Inc., Englewood Cliffs, N.J., 1971.

Goldstein, Robert J., **Introduction to the Cichlids**, TFH Publications, Inc., Englewood Cliffs, N.J., 1971.

Innes, William F., **Exotic Aquarium Fishes**, TFH Publications, Inc., Englewood Cliffs, N.J., 1971.

Jacobs, Kurt, **Livebearing Aquarium Fishes**, The MacMillan Co., N.Y., 1971.

Langler, Karl F., John Bardach, and Robert Miller, **Ichthyology**, John Wiley & Sons, Inc., N.Y., 1962.

Pet Library Guide Series, The Pet Library, Ltd., Harrison, N.J.

Scheel, Jorgen, **Rivulins of the Old World**, TFH Publications, Inc., Englewood Cliffs, N.J., 1968.

Schneider, Earl, **All About Breeding Tropical Fishes**, TFH Publications, Inc., Englewood Cliffs, N.J., 1966.

Spotte, Stephen H., **Fish and Invertebrate Culture**, John Wiley & Sons, Inc., N.Y., 1970.

Sterba, Gunther, **Aquarium Care—A Comprehensive Handbook**, Studio Vista Ltd. & E.P. Dutton & Co., Inc., Nexo leipzig, 1967.

Sterba, Gunther, **Freshwater Fishes of the World**, Vista Books, Longacre Press Ltd., London, 1963.

Stodola, Jiri, **Encyclopedia of Water Plants**, TFH Publications, Englewood Cliffs, N.J., 1967.

Zim, H.S. and H. Shoemaker, **Fishes**, Golden Press, N.Y., 1955.

INDEX

157

F G H I J